Reading Comprehension

Grade 3

Printed in the U.S.A.

ISBN 978-0-544-26767-1

4 5 6 7 8 9 10 0928 22 21 20 19 18 17 16 15

4500527565 A B C D E F G

Dear Parent,

Welcome to the *Core Skills Reading Comprehension* series! You have selected a unique book that focuses on developing your child's comprehension skills, the reading and thinking processes associated with the printed word. Because this series was designed by experienced reading professionals, your child will have reading success as well as gain a firm understanding of the necessary skills outlined in the Common Core State Standards.

Reading should be a fun, relaxed activity for children. They should read selections that relate to or build on their own experiences. Vocabulary should be presented in a sequential and logical progression. The selections in this series build on these philosophies to insure your child's reading success. Other important features in this series that will further aid your child include:

- Short reading selections of interest to a young reader.

- Vocabulary introduced in context and repeated often.

- Comprehension skills applied in context to make the reading more relevant.

- Multiple-choice exercises that develop skills for standardized test taking.

You may wish to have your child read the selections silently or orally, but you will find that sharing the selections and activities with your child will provide additional confidence and support to succeed. When learners experience success, learning becomes a continuous process moving them onward to higher achievements. Moreover, the more your child reads, the more proficient she or he will become.

Enjoy this special time with your child!

Sincerely,

The Educators and Staff of Houghton Mifflin Harcourt

Core Skills Reading Comprehension
GRADE 3

Table of Contents

Table of Contents
Core Skills Reading Comprehension, Grade 3

Skills Correlation

LANGUAGE ARTS SKILLS	SELECTION
COMPREHENSION	
Literary Texts	
*Answer Questions About Key Details	1, 4, 5, 6, 7, 8, 9, 11, 12, 14, 15, 16, 17
*Fables, Lessons, Themes	8, 9
*Characters	4, 9
*Word Meanings, Non-Literal Language	4, 7
*Text Structures (Chapter, Scene, Stanza)	1, 4, 5, Skills Review 1–5
*Point of View	4, 6
*Illustrations in Literary Texts	5, 8
*Compare and Contrast	9
Drawing Conclusions	15, 17, Skills Review 11–17
Perceiving Relationships	11, 12
Making Judgments	14, 16
Predicting Outcomes	16
Sequencing	9, 11, 12
Informational Texts	
*Answer Questions About Key Details	2, 3, 10, 13
*Answer Questions About Main Ideas and Supporting Details	2, 3, 13
*Textual Relationships	10, 11
*Word Meaning	2, 3, 10, 13
*Text Features and Search Tools	2, 5, 6
*Point of View	3
*Illustrations and Words in Informational Texts	2, 3
*Logical Connections	2, Skills Review 1–5
*Compare and Contrast Texts	3
Drawing Conclusions	13
Reading in the Content Areas	2, 3, 10, 14
Sequencing	10, Skills Review 6–10

* = Aligns to the Common Core State Standards for English Language Arts for grade 3

Skills Correlation, continued

LANGUAGE ARTS SKILLS	SELECTION
VOCABULARY	
*Word Meaning	1–4, 5–17
*Words in Context	9, 12
*Suffixes	7
Multiple Meanings	17
GRAMMAR AND USAGE	
Understanding Sentence/Paragraph Structure	7, 8, 10, 11
Combining and Identifying Phrases	7
When, *Where*, *Why*, and *How* Phrases	7, 10
*Agreement of Subject and Predicate	12
RESEARCH AND STUDY SKILLS	
*Using Beginning Dictionaries	5, 6
Understanding and Creating an Outline	13

* = Aligns to the Common Core State Standards for English Language Arts for grade 3

Vocabulary List

The selections are comprised of words carefully chosen from the Dolch Basic Sight Vocabulary and the Kucera-Francis word list. Words that appear most frequently in primary reading basal series were also used.

This vocabulary list includes important words from the selections and activities.

Selection 1
cheeks
fatter
furry
mumps
paw
rest
stripes
thin
tired
wait
whisper

Selection 2
doubled
gather
government
guide
president
trader
travel

Selection 3
canoes
decision
difficult
discoveries
explorer
governor
store
wilderness

Selection 4
climbed
gazed
ladder
mirror
neighborhood
promised
respect
sparkles

Selection 5
club
crack
fishbowl
joke
paint
save
settling
video

Selection 6
awful
boasted
bowl
busy
champion
equipment
helmet
hour
hurt
practice
protect
ramp
skateboard
stupid

Selection 7
base
bouncing
clumsy
giggle
muscles
praise
relax
relay
seriously
usually

Selection 8
appear
brought
enemies
hoof, hooves
lizard
protect
scarlet
skinny
sorry
taste

Selection 9
brag
capture
dare
mighty
porcupine
protection
quills
sharp
touch

Selection 10
camera
clever
crab
crack
diet
hatch
ocean
ooze
scientists
strong
submarine
tentacles

Selection 11
captain
crowded
engine
huge
leap
mainsail
passenger
sailor
thick
travel

Selection 12
crew
dawn
drift
several
stir
storm
sunrise
sunset

Selection 13
dinosaur
eagle
human
mammoth
million
mushroom
roach
swamp
swift
tear
world

Selection 14
break
bubble
evaporation
experiment
fact
interesting
magic
puddle
secret
soil
wind

Selection 15
cave-in
country
discovery
explore
mind
pasture
promise
straight
tease
tunnel

Selection 16
breakfast
burn
pack
push
ranger
slept
spark
stamp

Selection 17
check
followed
need
neighbor
panda
understand
whisper

Selection 1

1   The children had been at the big park all morning and all afternoon with Mack's father. They had gone on many rides and had seen many funny things. The hot September sun had made them tired. Some children were resting. They were waiting for Mack's mother to pick them up at six o'clock.

2   Kate said, "Look at that strange little animal."

3   They saw a tiny brown animal with black and white stripes down its back. It had a furry tail. Its tail was thinner than a squirrel's tail.

4   "That's a chipmunk," said Sandy, who was the oldest child. "Stay very still."

5   "Yes," whispered Joe. "Chipmunks are afraid of people. Don't let it know we are here."

6   The children watched the tiny animal run along the ground. Then it sat up on its back legs. It put its front paws up to its mouth. The chipmunk did this many times.

7   "I see something very strange," whispered Beth. "See how the chipmunk's face has changed!'

8   "Its cheeks are getting fatter and fatter!" said Ted.

9   The tiny animal's cheeks were all puffed up. Every time the chipmunk's paws went to its face, its cheeks got larger.

10   "I know why," said Ted. "It must have the mumps!"

11   "Poor, sick little chipmunk!" said Della.

12   "That's not why its cheeks are getting fatter!" said Sandy.

A **Underline the right answer.**

1. What is the selection about?

   a. how an animal's cheeks looked larger

   b. the chipmunk's home

   c. rides the children went on at the park

2. Why do you think the chipmunk's cheeks looked larger?

   a. It had the mumps.

   b. It was holding food in its mouth.

   c. It was blowing up balloon.

3. When was Mack's mother coming?

   a. at midnight   **b.** in the evening   **c.** at noon

4. How did the children feel after the day in the park?

   a. tired   **b.** smaller   **c.** furry

5. What do you think Mack's mother will do with the children?

   a. take them into the big park

   b. take them home

   c. help them catch the chipmunk

6. What did Ted and Della think was wrong with the chipmunk?

   a. It was hungry.

   b. It was not happy.

   c. It was sick.

7. What do we know about chipmunks?

   a. They have large noses

   b. They have fur on them.

   c. They have feet like birds.

8. What is a good name for this selection?

   a. Rides in the Park

   b. A Trip to the Zoo

   c. Watching the Chipmunk

Name _____ Date _____

B Detective Sharp Eye says, "You will need good eyes to know who is talking." Write the name next to the sentence.

1. Ann said, "A chipmunk has stripes." _____

2. "Della, what other tiny animal has stripes down its back?" asked Mack.

   _____

3. "That animal acts strange," whispered Mack. _____

4. "Stand still," said Joe, "because the chipmunk is afraid of us." _____

5. "Here comes the car now, Sandy," said Kate. _____

6. Now, look back at the selection on page 1. Who is talking in paragraph 2?

   _____

7. Who is talking in paragraph 7? _____

8. Who is talking in paragraph 10? _____

9. Who is talking in paragraph 5? _____

10. Who is talking in paragraph 12? _____

11. Who is talking in paragraph 11? _____

C Draw lines to match these.

1. small animal with fur   strange

2. talked very softly   resting

3. sitting quietly   furry

4. not as fat as   chipmunk

5. part of the face   oldest

6. thin lines of color   stripes

7. in need of rest   whispered

8. the first one born   thinner

9. different; not like others   cheek

                                        tired

D These marks " " are clues. They tell you what someone said. This mark " is just before the first word someone said. This mark " comes just after the last word someone said. Put a circle around any mark that is not in the right place in the sentences. One is done for you.

1. Joe ⓒsaid, Chipmunks are afraid of people."

2. "Is the chipmunk here?" asked Mack's mother in the car.

3. "Yes," said Della. "Look at the " sick little animal.

4. "Oh!" It has the mumps, Ted," said Sandy.

E Put these marks " " in the right places to show what is said. Then tell who is talking. If no one is talking, write *no one*.

1. Tomorrow I'm going to Bob's birthday party, said Joe.

   _____

2. Mack said, I'm going too. Let's get Bob something for his birthday.

   _____

3. I'm on my way to the store now, said Joe. Come with me.

   _____

4. Mack and Joe went to the toy store. They saw many toys to buy. They did not

   know what to get. _____

5. Then Joe saw a puzzle. He said, This is what I want to get for Bob.

   _____

6. I'll get this ant farm, said Mack, because Bob likes bugs.

   _____

7. But his grandmother won't let Bob keep bugs in the house, said Joe.

   _____

8. Bob likes to build things, said Mack. I'll get this race car and he can put

   it together. _____

Name _____ Date _____

F Read the play. What are Bird and Chipmunk talking about? Answer the questions. Write complete sentences for your answers.

Bird and Chipmunk

SCENE ONE

BIRD and CHIPMUNK are in a field.

BIRD: Hey Chipmunk! Your face looks funny! It is so fat. Do you have the mumps?

CHIPMUNK looks at Bird. He rolls his eyes.

BIRD: Why don't you answer me? What is wrong with you, Chipmunk?

CHIPMUNK walks across the grass. BIRD follows him.

BIRD: Poor, Chipmunk. You must be sick! You can't talk.

CHIPMUNK goes into his home in the ground.

BIRD: Well, that was rude!

SCENE TWO

CHIPMUNK climbs out of his house. He sees BIRD and smiles at her.

CHIPMUNK: I couldn't talk, Bird! I was picking up seeds. I store them in my cheeks.

BIRD: What a silly thing to do. Why not eat them now?

CHIPMUNK: I'm putting them away for winter.

BIRD: I'm never here in winter. I fly to the sunny south.

CHIPMUNK: Well, lucky you! I have to stay here in the cold.

BIRD: Why?

CHIPMUNK: I can't fly, Bird.

BIRD: Well, that's terrible! Do you need some help getting more seeds?

CHIPMUNK: Thank you, Bird! I'm ready for winter now.

BIRD: I'll see you in the spring.

CHIPMUNK: Bye, Bird!

BIRD flies away. CHIPMUNK smiles and waves.

Name _____ Date _____

1. What made Chipmunk's cheeks so fat? _____

_____

2. Where did Chipmunk take the seeds? _____

_____

3. Why must Chipmunk store seeds? _____

_____

4. Why doesn't Bird store food for winter? _____

_____

5. Why didn't Chipmunk talk to Bird at first? _____

_____

6. Which scene tells you why Chipmunk doesn't talk at first? _____

_____

7. What makes you think that this play isn't based on a true story? _____

_____

_____

8. Why can't Chipmunk go south? Underline the right answer.
   a. He is too poor.
   b. He is too big.
   c. He gets lost.
   d. He has no wings.

Name _____ Date _____

Selection 2: Paired

The Lewis and Clark Journey

In his first term as president, Thomas Jefferson nearly doubled the size of the United States in one move. He did this by buying a huge block of land from the French government. This land came to be called the Louisiana Purchase. The land stretched west from the Mississippi River to the Rocky Mountains.

President Jefferson asked his secretary, Meriwether Lewis, to head a trip to find out more about the new land. Lewis asked William Clark to lead the trip with him.

The plan was to travel up the Missouri River, walk to the Columbia River, and finally travel by boat to the Pacific Ocean. Along the way, Lewis and Clark would gather examples of plants and make notes about the animals. They would also meet the Native Americans who lived there.

In May of 1804, the trip started. In the fall, the group of explorers arrived at a Mandan Indian village. There were no maps to tell them where to go. They hired a French trader to guide them. The trader was with his Native American wife. Her name was Sacagawea. She was also a guide, but mostly, she helped the explorers talk to other the Native Americans.

After more than a year of exploring, the explorers reached the Continental Divide. This is the line at which the rivers start flowing west to the Pacific Ocean rather than east. They thought they would find the Columbia River, but they could see only mountain after mountain stretching before them. Just when finding the river seemed hopeless, the explorers met some Shoshone people. Sacagawea recognized one of the chiefs as her own brother. He sold the group many horses and found them a guide.

More than two years after they began their journey, Lewis and Clark arrived back at their starting point in St. Louis, Missouri. They had been gone a long time, so people were afraid that everyone had died on the trip. The news of their arrival made people very happy.

The Lewis and Clark trip was one of the most important journeys ever taken in this country. Lewis and Clark had made a map of the region. They also gave new information about the people, plants, and animals that lived there.

A **Underline the right answer.**

1. Which place was part of the Louisiana Purchase?

   a. France　　　　　　**b.** St. Louis　　　　　　**c.** the Columbia River

2. What did President Jefferson want Lewis to do?

   a. buy the land

   b. find out more about the land

   c. learn to speak Mandan Indian

3. Why did Lewis and Clark hire a guide?

   a. They could not read a map.

   b. They left their maps at home.

   c. There were no maps to show them where to go.

4. How long did the trip last?

   a. about six months　　　**b.** about one year　　　**c.** about two years

5. Who did the Shoshone people know?

   a. Sacagawea　　　　**b.** President Jefferson.　　　**c.** Meriwether Lewis

6. You want to find out more about the trip. Which words would be best to use for an Internet search?

   a. *President Jefferson*

   b. *Lewis and Clark trip*

   c. *Native Americans*

7. Look at the picture of Lewis and Clark. What tells you the trip happened a long time ago?

   a. the mountains

   b. the men's clothes

   c. the men's faces

8. What is the main idea of this selection?

   a. With help, Louis and Clark made an important journey.

   b. One of the people on the journey was Meriwether Lewis.

   c. There were no maps of the land long ago.

Name _____ Date _____

B **Look at the map. Then underline the right answer.**

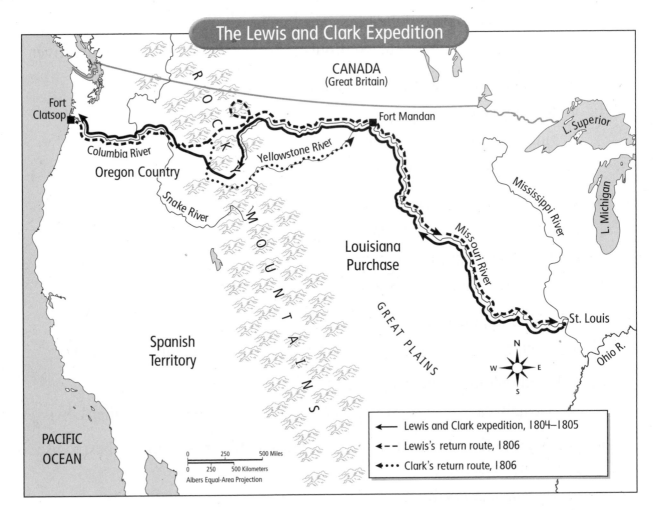

The Lewis and Clark Expedition

CANADA
(Great Britain)

Fort Clatsop

Columbia River

Oregon Country

Snake River

R O C K Y

Yellowstone River

M O U N T A I N S

Fort Mandan

Missouri River

Mississippi River

L. Superior

L. Michigan

Louisiana
Purchase

Spanish
Territory

GREAT PLAINS

St. Louis

Ohio R.

N W E S

PACIFIC
OCEAN

0   250   500 Miles
0 250   500 Kilometers
Albers Equal-Area Projection

⟵— Lewis and Clark expedition, 1804–1805
◂- - Lewis's return route, 1806
◂•••• Clark's return route, 1806

1. Look at the box at the bottom of the map. The word *route* means "way." What do the dotted lines tell you?

   a. where Lewis and Clark traveled

   b. how long it took Lewis and Clark to take the trip

   c. how many people Lewis and Clark took with them

2. Look at the dotted lines and arrows on the map. What kind of water did the group travel on?

   a. seas   **b.** rivers   **c.** lakes

Selection 2: Paired
Core Skills Reading Comprehension, Grade 3

C Writers can tell about events and people in different ways.

They can tell why something happened.
They can tell when something happened.
They can tell how two events or people are the same.

Put a ✓ by the sentence that describes the selection.

1. The trip started in 1804. One year later, the explorers reached the Continental Divide. Two years later, the explorers arrived back where they started.

   _____ **a.** It tells how people or events are the **same**.

   _____ **b.** It tells **when** events happened.

   _____ **c.** It tells **why** events happened.

2. Sacagawea was the sister of a Shoshone chief. Because the explorers were with his sister, the chief sold them horses.

   _____ **a.** It tells how people or events are the **same**.

   _____ **b.** It tells **when** events happened.

   _____ **c.** It tells **why** events happened.

3. A French trader was a guide. His wife was also a guide.

   _____ **a.** It tells how people or events are the **same**.

   _____ **b.** It tells **when** events happened.

   _____ **c.** It tells **why** events happened.

4. Lewis led the trip. Clark led it, too.

   _____ **a.** It tells how people or events are the **same**.

   _____ **b.** It tells **when** events happened.

   _____ **c.** It tells **why** events happened.

Selection 3: Paired

Lewis and Clark

An Exciting Job

In 1804, President Thomas Jefferson asked Meriwether Lewis to lead a daring journey. Lewis chose his good friend William Clark to lead with him. Lewis and Clark chose about 30 men with good wilderness skills. They wanted to find a safe water route, or way, to the Pacific Ocean. With high hopes, this group of explorers set off on a journey that lasted 28 months. The explorers started in St. Louis and headed up the Missouri River.

A Difficult Trip

The explorers traveled 7,600 miles and faced many difficulties on the way. When it got too rough, they left their large boats behind. Traveling over the Rocky Mountains was a hard part of the trip. The cold winter made it hard to find food and water. They were tired and hungry when they came out of the mountains. Luckily the explorers met friendly Native Americans who fed them and showed them how to build canoes.

Lewis and Clark made many discoveries. But who were these men who became American heroes?

Meriwether Lewis (1774–1809)

Meriwether Lewis was born on a farm in Virginia in 1774. He joined the United States Army and spent time on the frontier in Ohio and Tennessee. After seven years in the army, Lewis became a captain. He later worked for his friend, President Jefferson.

Because he had lived on the frontier, Lewis was the perfect choice to lead the journey. He made the plans for the main riverboat himself. He wanted to make sure it had enough room to store everything they would need for the journey. He brought along his dog, Seaman. Seaman was a great watchdog for the crew. Captain Lewis wrote about the trip in his journal every day. He wrote down all of the gifts they made to Native Americans they met along the way.

After the trip, Lewis became the governor, or leader, of the Louisiana Territory.

D These sentences tell information about the trip. Tell whether the information came from one of the selections or both of them. Write *ONE* or *BOTH*. One is done for you.

___**BOTH**___ 1. The trip started in 1804.

_____ 2. The Louisiana Purchase doubled the size of the United States.

_____ 3. Lewis and Clark were friends.

_____ 4. The trip lasted more than two years.

_____ 5. The trip was 7,600 miles long.

_____ 6. Lewis worked for President Jefferson.

_____ 7. Lewis and Clark were born in Virginia.

_____ 8. The trip began in St. Louis, Missouri.

_____ 9. Lewis and Clark took about 30 men on the trip.

_____ 10. Sacagawea was married to a French trader.

_____ 11. President Jefferson asked Lewis to make the trip.

_____ 12. The group met Native Americans on the trip.

Name _____ Date _____

E **Put a ✓ next to the right answer to each question.**

1. Which selection tells about the early lives of Lewis and Clark?

 _____ **a.** "Lewis and Clark's Journey"

 _____ **b.** "Lewis and Clark"

 _____ **c.** both selections

2. Which selection shows what Lewis and Clark looked like?

 _____ **a.** "Lewis and Clark's Journey"

 _____ **b.** "Lewis and Clark"

 _____ **c.** both selections

3. Which selection shows what Sacagawea looked like?

 _____ **a.** "Lewis and Clark's Journey"

 _____ **b.** "Lewis and Clark"

 _____ **c.** both selections

4. Which selection tells how many maps Clark drew?

 _____ **a.** "Lewis and Clark's Journey"

 _____ **b.** "Lewis and Clark"

 _____ **c.** both selections

5. Which selection tells what tribe Sacagawea was from?

 _____ **a.** "Lewis and Clark's Journey"

 _____ **b.** "Lewis and Clark"

 _____ **c.** both selections

Selection 4

Our Treehouse

The big oak tree stood in our yard
Like our father watching us play.
Father gazed up at its strong branches.
Reaching to the sky.
What could they hold?
"A treehouse," he said.

He climbed into the branches
And tied pieces in place with rope.
"The tree would be sad
If we used nails," he said.
First floor, then walls, and then
A house against the blue sky!
Then he unrolled a rope ladder
And climbed back down.

He said we could only use the treehouse
When he or mother was home.
We could not fight.
We had to treat the tree with respect.
We promised all these things.

Then we climbed the rope ladder.
Up into the branches.
We looked down
And saw a boy and girl.
It felt like looking in a mirror.

Father asked their parents
If they could play.
Now we all climb the rope ladder
Into the branches together.
We can see the whole neighborhood
And sometimes,
When the sky sparkles blue,
We can see the whole world.

Name _____ Date _____

1. What does the poet compare the oak tree to in the second line of the poem?

   a. a treehouse

   b. his father

   c. a friend

2. Why does the poet's father use rope to build the treehouse?

   a. He wants to protect the tree.

   b. He has run out of wood and nails.

   c. He wants to protect his children.

3. What do the poet and his sister promise to do?

   a. build a treehouse

   b. swing from the rope

   c. treat the tree with respect

4. What does the father do right after building the treehouse?

   a. He ties the floors and walls in place.

   b. He talks to the neighbors' parents.

   c. He makes rules for using the treehouse.

5. Why does the poet say seeing a boy and girl "felt like looking in a mirror"?

   a. The boy and girl are dressed the same.

   b. The boy and girl look like the poet and his sister.

   c. The boy and girl are holding a mirror up to the sky.

6. What is the main idea of the poem?

   a. A treehouse should be made out of rope.

   b. A father builds a treehouse for his son and daughter.

   c. Every child should have a treehouse.

7. Which word best describes the poet and his sister at the end of the poem?

   a. *silly*

   b. *friendly*

   c. *angry*

8. Which words tells you about the setting of the poem?

    a. *boy, girl, mirror*

    b. *father, climbed*

    c. *tree, yard*

9. When does the "sky sparkle blue"?

    a. at night

    b. during the day

    c. in a storm

10. Look at the treehouse on this page. How do you know it's <u>not</u> the treehouse the father build?

    a. It is in a big tree.

    b. It has nails.

    c. It is up high.

B **Some poems are broken into stanzas, or groups of lines. This poem has five stanzas. Match the description with the right stanza number.**

Stanza one

Stanza two

Stanza three

Stanza four

Stanza five

    a. Father makes the treehouse.

    b. The poet and his sister see another boy and girl.

    c. Father asks if the boy and girl can play in the treehouse.

    d. Father gives the rules.

    e. Father looks up at the tree and decides to make a treehouse.

Name _____ Date _____

C **Write the word from the box next to its correct meaning.**

gazed	ladder	neighborhood	sparkles
promised	climbed	mirror	respect

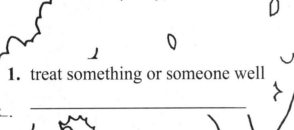

1. treat something or someone well

   _____

2. a place where people live

   _____

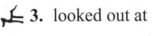

3. looked out at

   _____

4. glass that shows a picture
   of what is in front of it

   _____

5. went up

   _____

6. said you will do something

   _____

7. gives off light

   _____

8. something to use to climb

   _____

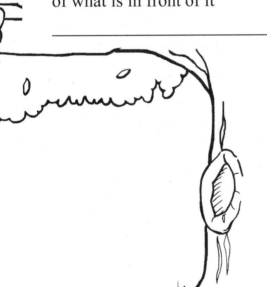

D Read each sentence. Decide which person or people from the poem would say it. Write the name of the person or people next to the sentence.

father	poet	sister	mother

1. I built a treehouse for my children. _____

2. My dad built a treehouse for my sister and me. _____

3. My brother and I sit in the treehouse. _____

4. I asked the parents of the boy and girl if they could play in the treehouse.

_____

5. My husband likes trees. _____

6. We promised our father we would not fight. _____

7. Our children like the treehouse. _____

E The poet likes the treehouse. Would you like your own treehouse? Tell why or why not.

_____

_____

_____

_____

_____

F **Use this table of contents from a book to answer the questions below.**

Table of Contents

1. What is the book about?

_____

2. In which part would you find a list of all the things you need to build a treehouse?

_____

3. Write the page numbers where you can find out about these.

_____ **a.** making the floor of a treehouse

_____ **b.** making a treehouse without nails

_____ **c.** keeping your treehouse clean

_____ **d.** staying safe in your treehouse

_____ **e.** putting a roof on your treehouse

Selection 5

Donna and her friends had a detective club. The children met every Thursday to read detective stories. The club was saving money to buy a new video detective game.

One Thursday afternoon, the club met at Ellen's house. The children put their money together on top of a table.

Ralph said, "Look at your baby brother, Ellen!"

The baby was painting the walls and a chair with Ellen's paints.

"Stop, Bert!" shouted Ellen. "Bert just learned how to climb out of bed by himself. Now he gets into everything!" Ellen picked up Bert.

Liz said, "I'll hold him."

"I'll put all the money away," said Donna, "so Bert can't grab it!"

Ellen gave Donna a big red wooden box for the money. Just then Bert pulled away from Liz. He bumped into the fishbowl. Water, bits of glass, and fish fell all over the floor. Then Bert grabbed the money from the table.

Donna took the money away from Bert. Then she ran into the kitchen with the box and the money. She opened the big box. Inside was a smaller box. Donna opened it. Inside that one was a very small box. Donna put the money in it.

As she was putting the boxes back together, the middle one fell. The lid got a crack in it. Donna hid the boxes in the kitchen.

Ralph was settling Bert in his bed for a nap. Ellen was cleaning off the paint. Mark was sweeping up the glass. Liz was putting the goldfish into a glass of water.

"Where is the money now?" asked Ellen.

Donna went into the kitchen to open the boxes. The money was gone.

"Who took the money?" Donna asked her friends. "It was right inside here!" She showed them the big box.

Ralph said, "Was it? Maybe you put it in the middle box, the one with the crack in the lid."

"Be like Detective Sharp Eye, Donna," said Liz.

"Let's see if you can find out who took it!" said Mark.

Then Donna knew. Her detective friends were playing a joke. They were trying to find out how good a detective she was.

Donna thought. At last, she said, "It can't be Ellen. She has paint on her hands. There is no paint on the box."

Donna said, "Mark cleaned up the wet bits of glass. Liz picked up the wet goldfish. But this box is dry. So we know they did not put their wet hands on the box."

"That leaves you, Ralph," said Donna. "Give me the money, please."

"I didn't take it," whispered Ralph. "Little Bert did."

"No, he didn't!" yelled Donna. "I knew you did it as soon as you said the middle box had a crack in it. I had just dropped it. No one but the person who took the money and I knew about the crack. I kept that middle box hidden in the big box to trap you!"

"Well, Donna, you've learned a lot from Detective Sharp Eye!" said all the children.

A **Underline the right answer.**

1. What is a good name for this selection?

   a. The Pretty Boxes

   b. Donna, a Good Detective

   c. Bert Learns to Paint

2. Why did someone take the money?

   a. to buy a paint set

   b. to buy more goldfish

   c. to see if Donna could think like a detective

3. When was the money taken?

   a. when the children were cleaning up

   b. before Bert made a mess

   c. when Donna was in the kitchen

4. How did Donna know who took the money?

   a. Liz told Donna who took the money.

   b. The child told about the crack in the middle box.

   c. Bert saw the child hide the money in the middle box.

5. What was the selection mostly about?

   a. a video game

   b. a baby who got into everything

   c. someone who could think like a detective

6. How did Donna know who had not taken the money?

   a. The boxes were clean and dry.

   b. The boxes had paint on them.

   c. The boxes were wet.

7. What does the picture with the selection tell you about Donna?

   a. She has friends.

   b. She likes the box.

   c. She wants to be a detective.

27

Name _____ Date _____

B A dictionary tells what words mean. The words in a dictionary are in
ABC order. This is called alphabetical order. Look at the picture dictionary.
Answer the questions.

Animals

donkey A donkey helps people work.

eagle An eagle is a large and strong animal.

hippopotamus A hippopotamus eats water plants.

kangaroo A kangaroo hops.

1. Which animal has feathers? Write the word. _____

2. If the word *lizard* were on this page, where would it be found?
   Underline the right answer.

   a. before *donkey*

   b. between *hippopotamus* and *kangaroo*

   c. after *kangaroo*

3. If the word *camel* were on this page, where would it be found?
   Underline the right answer.

   a. before *donkey*

   b. after *eagle*

   c. between *donkey* and *eagle*

Name _____ Date _____

C Read the play. Answer the questions that follow it. Write complete sentences for your answers.

The Puzzle

SCENE ONE

RALPH and ELLEN sit in the dining room. They work on a puzzle.

RALPH: Ellen, we have worked on this puzzle for two weeks!

ELLEN: I know, Ralph. It's been hard work. I've had fun, though.

RALPH: Me, too. But I'll be glad when it's done.

ELLEN puts the last piece in the puzzle.

ELLEN: It's done, Ralph! What a pretty picture! Let's get Mom to look at it.

RALPH and ELLEN walk to the kitchen. Baby Bert walks to the table. He pulls puzzle pieces off the table. They land on the floor.

BERT: Me play too!

SCENE TWO

MOM, RALPH, and ELLEN walk into the dining room. They find Bert on the floor playing with the puzzle pieces.

MOM: Oh, no! What a mess!

ELLEN: Bert! What did you do?

MOM: Ellen, I'll help you put it together again.

RALPH: That was two weeks of work! I'm so mad!

MOM: I bet you are! But remember, Bert is little. He doesn't know better. I'll put him in his playpen. He can watch us.

MOM, RALPH, and ELLEN pick up the puzzle pieces. They sit at the table and start putting the pieces back together.

Name _____ Date _____

1. What were Ralph and Ellen doing in Scene One? _____

_____

2. How long had the children worked on the puzzle? _____

_____

3. Why did Ellen and Ralph go out of the room? _____

_____

4. What will Mom do? _____

_____

5. What do you think Baby Bert would say at the end of Scene Two? Write what you think he would say.

_____

_____

D **Write the word that goes in each sentence. Use the words below.**

club	joke	sweeps	save
cleaned	cracked	shouted	

1. He _____ the floor to clean it.

2. The kitchen needs to be _____.

3. The _____ meets every Friday.

4. That _____ was funny!

5. Why don't you _____ your money until you need it?

6. When the egg fell on the floor, it _____.

Skills Review: Selections 1–5

A Use the table of contents to answer the questions below.

1. What is the book about? _____

2. Name four places where nests are found.

   _____ _____ _____ _____

3. Write the page numbers where you can find out about these.

   _____ **a.** a robin's nest in a tree

   _____ **b.** where a turkey builds a nest

   _____ **c.** nests near water

   _____ **d.** two places where insects build nests

   _____ **e.** where a chicken lays eggs

   _____ **f.** where duck eggs can be found

4. What kind of nests are in this book? Circle the answer.

   a. nests of snakes   **c.** nests of birds and insects

   b. nests of frogs and tadpoles   **d.** nests of fish

B Put a ✓ by the sentence that describes the selection.

1. Henry likes to tell jokes. He is a funny person. Sally tells funny stories, too. She makes her friends smile.

   _____ **a.** It tells how people or events are the **same**.

   _____ **b.** It tells **when** events happened.

   _____ **c.** It tells **why** events happened.

2. The family saw a chipmunk. Because it needed food for winter, it had fat cheeks.

   _____ **a.** It tells how people or events are the **same**.

   _____ **b.** It tells **when** events happened.

   _____ **c.** It tells **why** events happened.

3. In 2013, the father built a treehouse. The next year, a squirrel moved in.

   _____ **a.** It tells how people or events are the **same**.

   _____ **b.** It tells **when** events happened.

   _____ **c.** It tells **why** events happened.

4. On the trip to the farm, the class learned about animals. They learned about animals at the zoo, too.

   _____ **a.** It tells how people or events are the **same**.

   _____ **b.** It tells **when** events happened.

   _____ **c.** It tells **why** events happened.

Name _____ Date _____

C **A dictionary tells what words mean. The words in a dictionary are in ABC order. This is called alphabetical order. Look at the picture dictionary. Answer the questions.**

Toys

ball   You throw a ball.

doll   A doll is a toy that looks like a person.

kite   A kite flies in the air.

truck   A truck takes things from one place to another.

1. Which toy looks like a person? Write the word. _____

2. If the word *car* were on this page, where would it be found?
   a. before *ball*
   b. between *ball* and *doll*
   c. after *kite*

3. If the word *marbles* were on this page, where would it be found?
   a. after *ball*
   b. after *doll*
   c. before *truck*

D **Circle the right word.**

1. Someone who shows you where to go is a (governor, guide, gather).

2. The leader of the state is the (governor, gather, guide).

3. A boat you row is called a (cheek, canoe, club).

4. A part of your face is called your (club, canoe, cheek).

5. When something is hard, it is (difficult, decision, discovery).

6. A (doubled, discovery, difficult) is something a person finds.

7. If there are twice as many people in your class, the number of people (difficult, doubled, discovered)

8. You should go to bed soon if you are (trader, travel, tired).

9. A chipmunk will (gather, guide, governor) food for winter.

10. A chipmunk has (sparkles, stripes, stores).

E **Who is talking? Write the name next to the sentence.**

1. Lewis said, "It's time to go on a journey." _____

2. "Lewis, it is very cold out here!" said Clark. _____

3. "Sacagawea, can you help us?" asked Lewis. _____

4. Jefferson said, "Lewis, I want you to find out about the new land."

    _____

Read the play. Then answer the questions. Write complete sentences for your answers.

The Wilderness Club

SCENE ONE

TIM is in his living room. His friends KATE and JACK are with him.

TIM: This is the first meeting of our new club!

KATE: What is the club going to do? Are we going to play games?

JACK: Will we make a treehouse?

TIM: No! This is a wilderness club. We will go on a journey. We will explore. We can make a fire and stay the night. We can even get canoes!

KATE and JACK giggle.

JACK: But we are eight years old, Tim. Our parents will not let us explore on our own.

KATE: Plus, it's too cold!

TIM: Oh, dear. I didn't think of that.

KATE: Wait! It's not too late. I have an idea. Let's go to my house to get some things from my brother Lou. Then, we can go to the video store.

SCENE TWO

The three friends are back at Tim's. They have Lou's tent. Tim is sitting in Lou's canoe. They are all playing a video game.

JACK: This video game is great. It's just like being in the wilderness.

TIM: It's not really what I wanted.

KATE: I know. But it's a start. We can learn. When we are older, my brother Lou will let us use his canoe.

JACK: I have snacks!

TIM smiles.

TIM: Okay. Our first journey isn't so bad!

Name _____ Date _____

1. What kind of club does Tim want? _____

2. Why can't the three children do what Tim wants? _____

_____

3. Where does Kate get the tent and canoe? _____

_____

4. Where do the children have their first journey? _____

_____

5. What is the video game like? _____

6. Which scene tells you what Tim didn't think about? _____

7. Could this play be based on a real story? Give a reason.

_____

_____

8. At first, what does Jack want to do? Underline the right answer.
   a. make a canoe
   b. build a treehouse
   c. go to the wilderness

9. Who has snacks? Underline the right answer.
   a. Tim
   b. Jack
   c. Kate

10. Who plays the video game? Underline the right answer.
    a. all three children
    b. Lou
    c. the parents

Selection 6

Early in the summer, Mark got a new skateboard for his birthday. Since then, he had been on the skateboard every day. He did nothing but practice every hour that he was awake.

Mark's parents made sure that he learned to skateboard on their driveway, where it was safe. They told him that he must always wear long pants and shoes. They also gave him the right safety equipment. He had a helmet, kneepads, elbow pads, and gloves.

Mark was good at sports. In no time, he was better at skateboarding than his friends.

"I can't wait around for you snails to learn! I'm too good!" boasted Mark. "I'm going to the skateboard bowl where there are high ramps."

Soon Mark no longer saw his old friends. He was too busy at the ramp talking to the older boys and learning new tracks. The big boys taught him "kick turns," "wheelies," and "lip tricks."

Mark got better and better at skateboarding. Everyone said that he would be a champion some day.

But Mark was not a champion at home. He never helped with any of the work around the house or yard. He never answered when his parents talked to him. He acted as if his little sister Julie was not even there. He did not look at her, help her, or say a word to her.

His school friends did not want to be around Mark. He boasted about how great he was on the skateboard. He made fun of them all the time because they were not as good as he was.

37

Mark was so busy thinking of himself that he forgot his family was going to the beach for a week. When Dad reminded him to pack his swimsuit and fins, Mark was upset.

"I am not going to that stupid beach!" he shouted. "I do not want to do anything but skateboard!"

Mom shut her ears. She packed Mark's things, but she did not put in any of his skateboard equipment.

"We are going to the beach, and so are you," she told Mark.

Once he got to the beach, Mark had fun swimming, fishing, and learning to dive. He did not think much about skateboarding until the family went to a mall to shop. Mark saw that a smooth sidewalk went down a hill from the mall to the parking lot.

"That hill is perfect for skateboarding," he thought.

Then one day, Eric, a friend Mark had made at the beach, showed Mark his skateboard. Mark grabbed the board from Eric and headed toward the mall.

Eric tried to get his board back. "You can't skateboard," he said to Mark. "You don't have any equipment. You are not even wearing shoes."

But Mark kept going. When they got to the mall, he jumped on the board. He did not even look down the hill to see if there was anything or anyone in the way. ZOOM! ZOOM! Down he went! People jumped out of the way as Mark raced past.

There were some tiny stones on the sidewalk. Mark did not see them. BANG! The skateboard wheels hit the stones! Mark did a backward flip and smashed down on the sidewalk.

It was an awful day for Mark. When he woke up, he was in the hospital. He had two broken bones in his left arm, three broken bones in his right arm, and mashed toes on both his feet. The doctor told Mark that toes that get mashed from skateboarding without shoes are called "hamburger toes."

The doctor also said that many skateboarders break their elbow bones. These breaks are called "skateboard elbows."

"You're the champion!" the doctor said to Mark. "You've got not one, but two skateboard elbows."

A **Underline the right answer to each question.**

  1. What do we know about Mark?

   a. He helped his sister all the time.

   b. He boasted a lot.

   c. He liked to work in the garden.

   d. He did good work in school.

2. What is this selection mainly about?

    a. all the sports Mark liked

    b. a well-liked boy

    c. the water sports at the beach

    d. a boy who wanted to do only one thing

3. In no time, Mark learned to skateboard. What does *in no time* mean?

    a. very slowly   **c.** never learned

    b. very quickly   **d.** did not have time for

4. What did Mark think about going to the beach with his family?

    a. He did not want to go.

    b. He was ready to go.

    c. He did not want his sister to go.

    d. He did not want his mother to teach him to swim.

5. When Mark's mother "shut her ears," what did she do?

    a. She put on her earmuffs.

    b. She put on her earrings.

    c. She did not let Mark talk.

    d. She did not listen to what Mark said.

6. Why did Mark's parents make him practice in the driveway?

    a. It was safer.

    b. Mark did not like to leave home.

    c. Mark had to watch Julie.

    d. Mark was too little to go to the park.

7. When did Mark start going to the skateboard bowl with the ramps?

    a. before his birthday

    b. after he took Julie to the park

    c. after he could skate well

    d. when his friends became good skaters

8. What equipment did Mark use to protect himself?

   a. helmet, shirt, and shorts

   b. kneepads, socks, and shorts

   c. elbow pads, long pants, and vest

   d. helmet, kneepads, elbow pads, and gloves

9. Mark did not want to go to the beach. Why?

   a. He did not like to sit in the sun.

   b. He could not swim.

   c. He wanted to be with his friends.

   d. He wanted to skateboard all the time.

10. Why did Mark make fun of his old friends?

    a. They learned to skateboard faster than Mark did.

    b. They did not have on their safety equipment.

    c. They did not learn to skateboard as fast as Mark did.

    d. They did not learn to dive as fast as Mark did.

11. What was awful about the last day at the beach?

    a. It rained all day long.

    b. Mark had to sell his skateboard equipment.

    c. Mark hurt himself.

    d. Mark got in trouble for stealing a skateboard.

12. What helped Mark become so good at skateboarding?

    a. He practiced a lot.   c. Julie helped him.

    b. His father helped him.   d. He helped his friends learn.

13. Why did the doctor say Mark was a champion?

    a. Mark was a champion skateboarder.

    b. Mark was the champion of broken bones.

    c. Mark was the best at breaking skateboards.

    d. Mark was the best brother Julie could have.

B **To be a champion, you must practice. Here are some of the new words in the selection. Read the sentences, learn to read the words, and know their meanings. Then, you will be a champ. Circle the right word to finish each sentence.**

1. For every sport, people must have the right (everything, equipment, ending).

2. A helmet is used to protect a person's (heat, head, heard).

3. To be the best in anything is to be a (champion, change, chicken).

4. When you work very hard at learning something, you are (protecting, packing, practicing).

5. Every day has twenty-four (ours, hears, hours).

6. When children try hard at something, they get (better, butter, basket).

7. When something is very bad, we say it is (awful, elbow, always).

8. We do not like people who (both, boat, boast) too much.

9. A place without steps where you can go up and down is a (rack, ramp, read).

10. Mark had several broken (bones, boards, bowls).

11. A part of an arm is an (along, evening, elbow), and a part of a leg is a (kick, knee, free).

12. To be hard at work is to be (busy, bus, buzz).

13. Poor Mark! His skateboard hit some (stores, stars, stones), and he got (heard, her, hurt).

14. Mark was the champion of the skateboard (ends, elbows, every).

Name _____ Date _____

 Here is the table of contents of a book that Mark and his friends read to learn about skateboarding.

Zip, Zip, Up and Away

Each chapter of the book tells you something you should know about skateboarding. Read what Mark wants to learn. Which chapter will tell him what he wants to know? Write the chapter title and page number.

1. Mark wants to know how to skateboard on a ramp.

_____

_____

3. Mark wants to know whether it is safe to practice in a parking lot.

_____

_____

2. Mark wants to know what equipment he must put on.

_____

_____

4. Mark wants to know how to do a wheelie on his skateboard.

_____

_____

Name _____ Date _____

D Look at the table of contents on page 43. In which chapter would each paragraph below be found? After each paragraph, write the chapter title and the page number where the chapter begins.

1.　　　Here are the main styles of this sport. The <u>Streetstyle</u> skateboarder jumps over boxes, bars, or other things while doing tricks. The <u>Freestyle</u> skater skates on flat places while doing tricks. In <u>Ramp skating</u>, the skateboarder skates up on the ramp and does tricks on the top edge, or lip, of the ramp.

Table of Contents	
Title	**Page**
_____ . . . . ____	

2.　　　One thing to remember is never to ride in and out of traffic on very busy streets. Skateboards are good for moving fast but only in places where you will not be hit by vans, trucks, or cars. Remember that water and wheels do not mix. It is bad to ride into puddles. The quickest falls happen with wet wheels.

Table of Contents	
Title	**Page**
_____ . . . . ____	

3.　　　Make sure that your skateboard is always kept in good order. Never ride until you have checked that the wheels are clean and ready to roll. If it happens to start raining as you ride, stop and get off. Put your skateboard into a plastic bag so it will not get wet.

Table of Contents	
Title	**Page**
_____ . . . . ____	

4.　　　When you first start on your skateboard, find places that are good practice spots. Flat places, your own driveway, and dead-end streets near your home can let you have as much time as you need to become a good skateboarder. Some towns may close streets to traffic for a short time so that skaters have enough room to practice.

Table of Contents	
Title	**Page**
_____ . . . . ____	

Name _____ Date _____

E Answer the questions about the table of contents and the dictionary.
Write *Table of Contents* or *Dictionary*.

Table of Contents   or   **Dictionary**

Stories

The New Skateboard . . . 2
A Surprise 4
Skateboard Tricks 7
The Fence Fell 10

1. Which one is in alphabetical order? _____

2. Which one has meanings of words? _____

3. Which one has chapters? _____

4. Which one tells how to say a word? _____

5. Which one tells the page on which a story begins? _____

F If you were one of Mark's old friends, and he had boasted and called you a snail, would you forgive him after he was hurt so badly? Would you go over to help him? Write three sentences telling how you would feel. Tell why you would feel that way.

_____

_____

_____

_____

_____

_____

G Remember that point of view is what someone thinks or feels about what happens. For example, one character might be happy about a birthday party. Another character might be upset because she wasn't asked to the party.

Think about Mark's story. Read the different points of view. Think about which character from the box would have that point of view. Then write the character's name under the point of view. In box 6, write your point of view about an event in the story. Put your name on the line beside the number.

Mark	Julia	Mom	Dad	Eric

I don't want to hear my son complain. I'm going to pack his bag. 1. _____	My friend just took my skateboard! He won't listen to me. He's going to get hurt! 4. _____
I want to ride my skateboard whenever I want. I'm the best skateboarder of all my friends. 2. _____	I asked Mark to pack his swimsuit. He got really upset and yelled at me! 5. _____
My brother acts like I'm not even here. He's being pretty mean. 3. _____	_____ _____ 6. _____

Selection 7

As the class lined up to go to the gym, Emily's heart started to beat faster. She kept saying to herself, "I hate gym. I hate gym."

Emily just was not very good at sports. She tried, but somehow she always did something that made some of the glass giggle and some feel sorry for her.

When they played softball, Emily always struck out. She had trouble catching, too. The ball seemed to slip right through her fingers.

Even when she did catch the ball, Emily had trouble throwing it to a player on a base. It usually ended up somewhere out in the field.

Emily thought about this as gym class started. At first, all went well. Mrs. Perkins, the gym teacher, had the children bouncing balls and running in place. No one could see who was doing well and who was not.

Then Mrs. Perkins divided the class into teams. Each member of a team had to take a turn climbing a rope. Emily got in line and waited for her turn.

Tony was in line behind Emily. "Let's see what you're going to mess up today, Emily," he said quietly. Tony did not want Mrs. Perkins to hear him. She took gym seriously. No laughing! No fooling around! No teasing!

Emily froze. She knew in her heart that Tony was right. She was clumsy. She was going to do something awful. It happened every time.

Emily's best friend, Letty, whispered, "Don't listen to mean old Tony. All you have to do is try to go up the rope a little way. Then just put one hand under the other and come down slowly."

Emily nodded. It was her turn. Mrs. Perkins said, "You can do it, Emily. Don't try too hard. Relax. Climb as high as you feel you can."

Emily went to the rope. She knew she was not good at climbing, but she would try. She thought she could get almost to the top. She started climbing. Up she climbed, like a monkey. She was halfway to the top.

The watching class cheered, "Go, Em, go! Good! Good!"

Emily was pleased by their praise. She relaxed. She slid to the floor.

Several days later, a new boy named Justin entered Emily's class. Justin was tall. He had big muscles and looked as if he would be good at sports. Everyone liked him because he was fun and kind.

"Just wait until Justin sees me in gym, Letty," Emily said. "He'll be making fun of me, too."

On the first gym day for Justin, the class did rolls and handstands on the mats. Cold with fear, Emily did everything without a slip. The class cheered.

When it was Justin's turn, Mrs. Perkins smiled as he came to the mat. Then, as she watched Justin, Mrs. Perkins looked puzzled.

It seemed Justin could not do a forward roll. He froze. He could do a backward roll, but when he tried a handstand, he flopped over.

Next, the class had relay races. Emily raced all the way quickly, picked up the beanbag, and started back to her team. She was almost there when she tripped and fell. She slid to her team, holding the beanbag in front of her.

"At least she got here!" shouted Letty, grabbing the beanbag and running.

The races ended suddenly when Justin tripped on his own shoe and slid into his team. He knocked them all down.

Justin and Emily both felt bad. Now no one would want either of them on their team.

"That leaves us two together," said Justin. "The last ones chosen."

Emily smiled. It was good to have company. It was better to have a friend.

A **Underline the right answer to each question.**

1. What was Emily's trouble?

    a. She did not think.

    b. She was sick all the time.

    c. She had no friends.

    d. She was clumsy.

2. What is the best meaning for the word *usually*?

    a. most of the time

    b. seldom

    c. once in a while

    d. never

3. What is the word for a kind of <u>laugh</u>?

    a. smile   **b.** frown

    c. praise   **d.** giggle

4. Why did everyone think Justin would be good at sports?

    a. He was fun to play with.

    b. He was kind.

    c. He had big muscles.

    d. He never made mistakes.

5. What happened when Emily climbed the rope?

    a. She could not climb up on the rope.

    b. She got stuck at the top.

    c. Letty had to bring Emily down.

    d. She went up well but came down too fast.

6. What could Justin do?

    a. climb a rope

    b. a backward roll

    c. a handstand

    d. a forward roll

Name _____ Date _____

B **Be a good sport. Hit a home run by writing each word next to its correct meaning.**

praise	bounce	relay
usually	relax	clumsy
serious	giggle	muscles

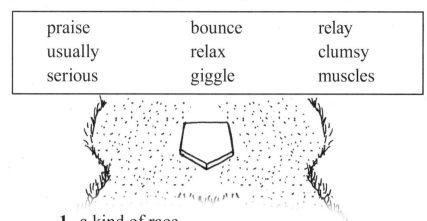

1. a kind of race _____

2. not funny _____

3. to tell how well you do
_____

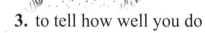
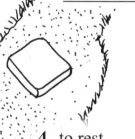

7. always dropping things
_____

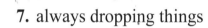

4. to rest
_____

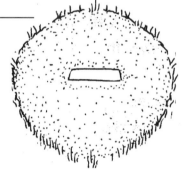

8. what a ball does
_____

5. most of the time _____

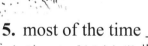

6. things that help your body move _____

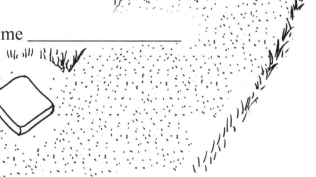

Selection 7
Core Skills Reading Comprehension, Grade 3

C Every sentence must have two parts: a *who* or *what* part and an *action* part. Read these sentences and underline the *who* or *what* part. Circle the *action* part.

1. Justin can practice.

2. Emily shouted.

4. Up, up, went the basketball.

You may add other words or phrases to a sentence to tell *when*, *where*, *why*, or *how* something happened.

D A *when* phrase tells the time that the action happens. Read to find out when the action happened. Finish each sentence with a *when* phrase from the box.

at night	in the morning	in the afternoon

1. Mrs. Bell left the party at midnight. Mrs. Bell was driving

   _____.

2. Letty walked home from school at three o'clock. She walked home

   _____.

3. The boys and girls played ball before school. They played

   _____.

E A *where* phrase tells the place where the action happened. Write the *where* phrases in these sentences.

1. Julie did a headstand on the mat. Where did Julie do the headstand?

   _____

2. The gym was on the first floor. Where was the gym?

   _____

Name _____ Date _____

F **Read to find out what Emily and Justin did to become less clumsy. Write the phrases from the sentences that answer the questions.**

The Rest of the Story

1. Every Thursday and Friday, Emily and Justin took swimming lessons at Garza Middle School.

   Who or What? _____

   Action? _____

   Where? _____

   When? _____

2. Emily learned to dive into the pool during her second lesson.

   Who or What? _____

   Action? _____

   Where? _____

   When? _____

3. Every morning, Justin does sit-ups in his bedroom.

   Who or What? _____

   Action? _____

   Where? _____

   When? _____

4. Justin's parents took many pictures on the playground the last day of school.

   Who or What? _____

   Action? _____

   Where? _____

   When? _____

Name _____ Date _____

G A *why* phrase tells the reason that the action happened. Complete the sentence by circling the *why* phrase that makes sense.

1. I turned on the lights _____.

       to see better   to hear better

2. He got the skates _____.

       to eat dinner   to have fun

3. She put on her helmet _____.

       to protect her elbows   to protect her head

4. Mom turned up the radio _____.

       to hear better   to see better

H A *how* phrase tells in what way an action was done. The pictures below show how some actions happened. Complete each sentence by writing the correct *how* phrase.

1. Marcos eats ice cream _____.

       with his tongue   with a fork

2. Sue bangs the drums _____.

       with two sticks   with her hands

3. The man swims _____.

       in the sea   in a pool

Name _____ Date _____

 1 Write the answers to the questions below. Then put the parts together to make a good sentence. Write the whole sentence on the lines. Start each sentence with a capital letter and end it with a period.

for food	all over the world	kill insects
in the spring	many birds	

When? _____

Who or What? _____

Where? _____

Action? _____

Why? _____

Sentence: _____

_____

across town	every morning	many children
travel	to reach the school	by car and bus

When? _____

Who? _____

Action? _____

Where? _____

How? _____

Why? _____

Sentence: _____

_____

Name _____ Date _____

J **Here is the end of the selection. Read it and write the correct phrase after each question.**

Emily swims and dives twice a week. In the water, she never trips and falls. She swims to help her become less clumsy. Justin still does sit-ups in the morning and in the evening. He practices to make his muscles strong.

1. Why does Emily swim so much? _____.

   to become clumsy   to become less clumsy

2. Where is Emily less clumsy? _____.

   in the water   in the gym

3. When does Emily swim and dive? _____.

   once a week   twice a week

4. How does Justin keep his muscles strong? _____.

   by doing sit-ups   by climbing ropes

5. Why does Justin keep his muscles strong? _____.

   to not trip   to get better at sports

6. When does Justin practice? _____.

   twice a day   three times a week

Selection 8: Paired

Lita was sad. The other lizards always crept away when Lita appeared on the tree bark.

"Don't come near us," the lizards said. "You bring our enemies around. They want to eat us."

Lita knew they were right. All the lizards were green, yellow, brown, or tan. All but Lita. She was strange.

Most lizards changed colors to match the trees and leaves where they lived. All but Lita. She could change colors like her friends, but her colors were bright and beautiful.

Most of the time, Lita was a beautiful pink. People, birds, and raccoons came crowding around to look at this pretty, strange lizard.

This upset Lita, so her pink changed to scarlet. If she became very, very, VERY upset, she turned bright purple. If there was a cool breeze, her purple color got light blue spots on it.

Many people said, "Oooh, ahhh! What beautiful colors."

Sometimes when animals came to see Lita, they would spot other lizards trying to hide in the leaves. Then they ate a good meal of lizards.

"You brought our enemies here," shouted the other lizards. "But we're the ones that will get gobbled up."

It was true. No animal would taste Lita. Her bright colors made them sick.

57

All alone, Lita felt unloved and unwanted. Even her mother would not come near her.

She was getting very skinny, too. It seemed that even insects went the other way when they spotted the bright lizard. Her long, thin, quick tongue could not catch any insects for food.

"I will ask some other animals how they protect themselves," said Lita. "Then I might be able to help my lizard friends. They might like me again."

First she went to the owl and asked him. He showed her his sharp claws and big beak. No help there!

Then she talked to the goat. He showed her his hard hooves that let him run very fast.

"I have this, too!" he yelled and tried to butt Lita with his sharp horns.

"Some lizards have horns, too," said Lita, "but ours cannot hurt other animals."

The next day Lita asked Mrs. Skunk, "How do you keep your enemies away, Mrs. Skunk?"

Mrs. Skunk laughed. "I'll show you," she said.

Lita was sorry she had asked. Why?

A **Underline the right answer to each question.**

1. What is this selection mainly about?

   a. the work of some lizards

   b. how owls protect themselves

   c. a strange lizard

   d. how skunks protect themselves

2. How did Lita feel when she was left alone?

   a. happy and free

   b. unloved and unwanted

   c. beautiful

   d. crowded

3. How did the lizards try to protect themselves?

   a. by butting their enemies with their horns

   b. by using their sharp claws

   c. by using a bad smell

   d. by matching the colors of trees and leaves

4. The pictures on pages 57 and 58 show two characters in the selection. What do the pictures tell you about the characters?

   a. They are happy.

   b. They are mad.

   c. They are animals.

   d. They are people dressed as animals.

5. Why was Lita getting skinny?

   a. She was on a diet.

   b. She was not hungry.

   c. All the insects went the other way.

   d. The goat told her not to eat.

6. How do lizards use their tongues?

   a. to clean themselves

   b. to capture food

   c. to tell their families of danger

   d. to climb trees

7. What is a lizard's tongue like?

   a. thick and strong and pink

   b. covered with fuzz

   c. long, thick, and flat

   d. long, thin, and fast

8. Lita turned scarlet. What color is that?

   a. bright blue   **c.** bright red

   b. light pink   **d.** bright purple

9. When did this selection happen?

   a. last year   **c.** on a winter evening

   b. last week   **d.** The selection does not tell.

10. Why didn't other lizards want Lita to come near them?

   a. They said she was too beautiful.

   b. Their enemies came to look at her.

   c. She was mean to them.

   d. She gobbled up her friends.

11. What is the best title for this selection?

   a. Loved by All

   b. Nobody's Friend

   c. The Animal with Hooves

   d. Lita's Horns

12. What happened last?

   a. Lizards crept away from Lita.

   b. People said, "Oooh, ahhh!"

   c. Lita's beautiful colors brought many enemies near.

   d. Lita talked to a skunk.

B Find the right word for each meaning. Write the words.

capture	strange	hooves	beautiful
crept	gobbled	taste	beak
brought	protect	enemies	

1. took something to a friend _____

2. to catch and hold _____

3. to see if something is good to eat _____

4. hard parts on goats' feet _____

5. to take care of _____

6. ate fast _____

7. odd, different _____

8. a part of a bird _____

9. very pretty _____

10. those who want to harm _____

C Let's learn about paragraphs.

1. Where does a paragraph start? The first word of a paragraph is moved to the right. We say it is indented. Look back at the selection on pages 57 and 58. How many paragraphs does the selection have?

   Write the number. _____

2. Write the first word in paragraph five. _____

3. Write the number of the paragraph that tells what colors the other lizards were.

   _____

4. Write the number of the paragraph that tells what happened when Lita got cold.

   _____

Name _____ Date _____

D Some words have a part added to them that changes their meaning. If these parts are added to the beginning of the words, they are called prefixes.

In this selection, we used the prefix *un*. *Un* means "not." See how the prefix changes the meaning of these words you know.

tied

untied

The words in the box have prefixes. Complete each sentence with the correct word.

unloved	unafraid	unanswered
unread	unseen	uneaten
unkind	unlocked	unchanged

1. The door was open. It was _____.

2. No one wanted the old doll. She was now _____.

3. The telephone rang and rang. It went _____.

4. The needles on the pine tree stayed green. They were

    _____.

5. The other lizards were mean to Lita. They were _____.

6. No one else would go near the horse, but Patty was _____.

7. Bob and Joe ate half the pie. The rest of the pie was

    _____.

8. The ducks did not know the hunters were there. The hunters were

    _____ in the bushes.

9. The books were locked in the trunk. They were _____.

Selection 8: Paired
Core Skills Reading Comprehension, Grade 3

Name _____ Date _____

E The main idea of a paragraph tells what the paragraph is about. Most of the information in the paragraph will be about one important idea.

Read the paragraphs. Answer the questions by placing a ✓ next to the correct answer.

1.   Some lizards have tongues that not only taste food but also smell it. When lizards see food, their long, slender tongues pop out. The tongue is very sticky. Once a bug is caught, it cannot get away.
What is this paragraph mainly about?

_____ **a.** kinds of foods lizards eat

_____ **b.** the mouths of lizards

_____ **c.** how lizards use their tongues

2.   A lizard has three parts. It has a head. It has a long body. It also has a tail. The body is held up on four short legs. Each foot has five toes on it. The toes help the animal stick to branches and tree trunks.
What is this paragraph mainly about?

_____ **a.** how lizards travel

_____ **b.** what a lizard's body is like

_____ **c.** where lizards live

3.   There are many insects found in the warm places where most lizards live. Lizards make bugs their main food. Sometimes it is hard to capture quick, little insects. Then a hungry lizard may even chew on leaves or flowers.
What is this paragraph mainly about?

_____ **a.** a lizard's shape

_____ **b.** a lizard's home

_____ **c.** a lizard's food

F Most paragraphs have a topic sentence that states the main idea. The other sentences in the paragraph give details that tell more about the main idea. Read the paragraphs. Find the topic sentences. Sometimes a topic sentence may be the first sentence. Sometimes a topic sentence may be the last sentence.

Underline the topic sentence in each paragraph.

1. Owls are the greatest mouse and rat hunters in the world. When owls look for food in the dark, their big eyes can spot rats and mice moving about. The owl swoops down to catch the smaller animal in its claws. Then it swallows it whole. Farmers love owls because they kill so many rats and mice.

2. Goats do not like to be fenced in. They try to get out of any place they are put in. They want to be free to snoop. They climb rocks and taste every bush they find. They see what they can discover in piles of trash and garbage. They snack on everything. Goats are interesting, funny animals.

G Read the paragraphs in F again. Copy each topic sentence. Under the topic sentence, write two details that give more information about the main idea.

Topic sentence 1 _____

_____

1. _____

2. _____

Topic sentence 2 _____

_____

1. _____

2. _____

Selection 9: Paired

About a week later, Lita was still trying to find a good way to protect herself. She couldn't change her colors to match the trees and leaves like the other lizards.

Lita saw a strange forest animal. It was covered with sharp quills.

"I'm a porcupine," he bragged. "We are mighty animals in these woods. We are left alone. No one dreams of eating us. No one dares to hit us."

"You are lucky," said Lita.

"Just give me a little touch with your long tail," said the porcupine.

Lita shook her head. She turned scarlet because she was so afraid.

"Make me angry!" begged the porcupine. "I can't stick you if I'm not mad."

Just then Lita unrolled her long, thin tongue to capture a passing fly. Seeing Lita stick out her tongue made the porcupine turn his back in anger. He backed up to a small bush. He bumped into the bush.

Lita turned purple! A porcupine quill stuck in every place his back touched.

"You are strong, mighty, and safe from enemies!" said Lita.

Lita heard noises nearby. Beavers were chopping down a large tree. Lita stared! The beavers were chopping with big, strong teeth.

"Do not listen to that bragging porcupine," said Mrs. Beaver. "If you want safety, come visit us."

Mrs. Beaver showed Lita how her family worked together. They found a stream. The beavers bit down trees and cut the wood into small pieces. Out of the wood they made a strong wall called a dam. The dam cut off part of the stream. That part of the water became a still pond where beaver families could live safely.

"We build strong houses in this pond," bragged Mrs. Beaver. "We can live under the water. No one touches us in this safe pond."

Mrs. Beaver began to bang her flat tail on the ground. She had seen danger. Some people were near. All the other beavers stopped working. Into the water they plopped. In ten seconds, every beaver was under the water, safe from enemies.

Lita knew she could not bang her tail like a beaver. She did not have quills like the porcupine. She could not let out a bad smell like a skunk. She did not have sharp claws like an owl or horns like a goat.

Then Lita looked into the pond for her beaver friends. What did she see? She saw a beautiful, bright pink animal looking up at her.

"Is that me?" asked Lita. "Why, I am beautiful!"

Lita now knew that her beauty was her protection from enemies. She did not have to be like a beaver, porcupine, skunk, owl, goat, or other lizards. She could just be herself! She did not feel sad anymore.

A **Underline the right answer to each question.**

1. What protects a porcupine?

   a. a sharp tongue

   b. sharp quills

   c. hooves on feet

   d. a flat tail

2. Why did Mrs. Beaver slap her tail on the ground?

   a. She was protecting her enemies.

   b. The tree was falling down.

   c. It was dinner time.

   d. She knew danger was near.

3. Why did the porcupine get mad at Lita?

   a. He thought Lita stuck her tongue out at him.

   b. Lita bragged about how strong she was.

   c. Lita turned purple.

   d. Lita was a friend of the beaver.

4. When do porcupines use their quills?

   a. when they are sleepy

   b. when they are angry

   c. when they are hungry

   d. when they are happy

5. How do porcupines move to protect themselves?

   a. from side-to-side

   b. rolled into a ball

   c. forward

   d. backward

6. Why do beavers make dams?

    a. to capture many fish

    b. to clean their teeth

    c. to have food for the winter

    d. to have a safe place for their homes

7. What is the main idea of this selection?

    a. A lizard has no way of protecting itself.

    b. Each kind of animal has a different way to protect itself.

    c. All animals protect themselves in the same way.

    d. All animals living in ponds are safe from enemies.

8. Why didn't Lita know she was beautiful?

    a. No one told her.

    b. The beaver said she was ugly.

    c. She had never seen herself before.

    d. The porcupine said she was ugly.

9. What happened last?

    a. The beavers popped into the pond.

    b. The porcupine hit the bush.

    c. Lita saw herself in the pond.

    d. Lita did not want to touch the porcupine.

10. What was Lita's protection from enemies?

    a. her tongue   **c.** the beaver's home

    b. her horns   **d.** her bright colors

11. What would happen if Lita dared to touch the porcupine?

    a. Quills would stick her.

    b. The porcupine would be scared.

    c. She would change into a porcupine.

    d. Nothing would happen to her.

B Finish each sentence with a word from the box.

scarlet	bragged	dare
anger	shook	touch
begged	quills	dam

1. The beavers' _____ was a wall to hold back water.

2. If we want to be safe, we would not _____ to cross a street without looking for cars.

3. Lita _____ her friends to stay with her.

4. The _____ were sharp stickers.

5. The strong woman _____ that she could lift a car by herself.

6. The flags were white and _____ .

7. The porcupine turned his back in _____ .

8. If you _____ a porcupine, it feels prickly.

C The prefix *un* means "not." Write the prefix *un* before each of these words to change their meaning.

a. _____ opened   c. _____ changed   e. _____ afraid
b. _____ covered   d. _____ locked

Match each word to its meaning. Write the letter of each new word on the line next to its meaning.

1. not scared   _____

2. stayed just the same   _____

3. never been opened   _____

4. opened up with a key   _____

5. took the quilt off   _____

Name _____ Date _____

Read the paragraph about fables. Then answer the questions.

A fable is a special kind of story. The characters in a fable are not people. They are animals. The animals speak like people. Sometimes, they act or feel like people, too. Fables teach a lesson. Often, the lesson is something that one of the animals in the story learns.

Think about the fable about Lita you read on pages 65 and 66.

1. What lesson does Lita learn in this fable?

   a. She needs to be more like the beavers.

   b. She doesn't have to change to protect herself.

   c. She should be nicer to other animals.

   d. She should hide her beauty to protect others.

2. These sentences tell about fables. Write an example from the selection about Lita for each sentence.

   a. Fables have animal characters.

   _____

   _____

   b. The animals in fables speak.

   _____

   _____

   c. The animals in fables act or feel like people.

   _____

   _____

Name _____ Date _____

E Read the selection. Then answer the question at the bottom of the page.

Cutting Down Trees

Before building homes, beavers always make a dam. First, they must cut down trees. Each beaver chews at a different tree. The beaver chews all around the tree trunk.

When the branches of a tree begin to shake, the beaver working on that tree slaps its tail on the ground. That tells the others to get out of the way so they will not be crushed by the falling tree.

Two or three more bites and the tree is down.

Now the group must chop the large tree into smaller pieces. They use their strong teeth for this job, too.

How does a beaver chop down a tree? Put the steps in the right order. One is done for you.

    a. The tree shakes a little.

    b. Other beavers get out of the way.

    c. The tree falls.

    d. The beaver takes the last bite.

    e. The beaver chews all around the tree trunk.

    f. The beaver warns the others.

1. **The beaver chews all around the tree trunk.** _____

2. _____

3. _____

4. _____

5. _____

6. _____

F When did these things happen? Write the word *before* or *after* on the line for each phrase. One is done for you.

1. When did the beavers build a dam?

   _____**before**_____ they built a house

2. When did the tree fall?

   _____ beavers got out of the way

3. When do the branches start to shake?

   _____ the tree is ready to fall

4. When does a beaver slap its tail on the ground to warn others?

   _____ the tree comes down

5. When do beavers chew a tree into smaller pieces?

   _____ the tree falls

G Synonyms are words that mean almost the same thing. *Small* and *little* are synonyms. Can you find the synonyms below? One is done for you.

1. big   a. close
2. mighty   b. quick
3. near   c. large
4. rocks   d. stones
5. woods   e. angry
6. fast   f. forest
7. mad   g. strong

H **When you compare and contrast, you tell how two stories are the same and different. Read each sentence. If the detail is in both Selection 8 and Selection 9, write *same*. If it is only in one selection, write *different*. One is done for you.**

1. The animals talk to each other. _____**same**_____

2. Lita is a lizard. _____

3. Lita talks to Mrs. Skunk. _____

4. Lita talks to Mrs. Beaver. _____

5. The other lizards stay away from Lita. _____

6. Lita is beautiful. _____

7. Lita learns how to protect herself. _____

8. Lita asks questions. _____

9. Lita's mother will not come near her. _____

10. Lita wants to know how to protect herself. _____

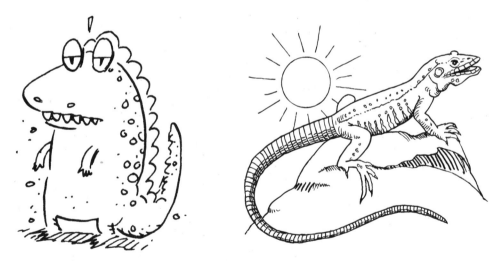

These pictures are the **same**. They are both lizards.
They are also **different**. One looks more like a real lizard.

1 **Here are some details about the selections. Write the letter and each detail in the correct box.**

    a. The selection takes place in a forest.

    b. The theme is learning you do not need to change.

    c. The theme is feeling different from others.

    d. Lita learns that some animals have horns.

    e. Lita learns that she is beautiful.

    f. The characters are all animals.

    g. All the animals speak.

    h. Lita meets a porcupine.

    i. Lita talks to a goat.

Selection 8	Both Selections	Selection 9

Selection 9: Paired
Core Skills Reading Comprehension, Grade 3

Selection 10

An octopus is a clever animal that lives in the ocean. It has a round body and two big eyes. The octopus is famous for having eight arms called tentacles. If one of its arms breaks off, it grows a new one!

Most octopuses live on the bottom of the ocean. They live in all the oceans of the world. They like warm waters best.

The octopus likes to live alone. Sometimes, it makes a home in cracks between large rocks. It can slide into the crack in the rocks. It can ooze out of the crack when it wants to get food or swim.

A female octopus lays thousands of eggs. She might lay them in holes or under rocks. She will stay close to them to make sure they are safe. It takes about six weeks for a baby octopus to hatch, or come out of the egg. When the babies hatch, they rise to the top of the water. Fish eat some of them. Others go back to the bottom of the ocean.

An octopus will use its tentacles to walk, to get food, and to swim about in the water. An octopus's diet includes crabs and clams. It picks the food up with its tentacles and pulls it into its mouth.

Scientists decided to see if the octopus would play. They put octopuses in an empty tank to see what they would do. The scientists put an empty pill bottle in the water. Soon, the octopuses were playing with the bottle.

Scientists can teach an octopus to open jars. First, scientists get in the tank and show the octopus how to take off the lid. The octopus then puts its body on the lid. It grabs the jar with its tentacles. It gets the lid off on its own by twisting its body over and over again. It can take an octopus up to an hour to open a jar. People have taken pictures with cameras of octopuses opening jars.

An octopus in a tank will often cause trouble. The octopus is strong as well as clever. It can take things apart. Someone once put a toy submarine in a tank. An octopus took it apart! An octopus can also get out of tanks. One octopus in England started getting out of its tank at night. It would go to another tank and eat the lumpfish. It took scientists several nights to learn who was eating the lumpfish!

Ⓐ Underline the right answer to each question.

1. Where do most octopuses live?

   a. the bottom of the ocean

   b. on the shore near the ocean

   c. at the top of the ocean

   d. on a ship in the middle of the sea

2. Where might an octopus make its home?

   a. inside a glass jar

   b. under a boat

   c. on the beach

   d. in a small crack in rocks

3. What are tentacles?

   a. the eyes of an octopus

   b. the legs of a whale

   c. the arms of an octopus

   d. the cameras of scientists

4. Why did scientists put an octopus in a tank with a pill bottle?

   a. to watch it open the bottle

   b. to see if it would play with the bottle

   c. to see if it could get out of the tank

   d. to watch it take the bottle apart

5. How many eggs does a female octopus lay?

   a. ten

   b. fifteen

   c. hundreds

   d. thousands

6. What is the first thing an octopus does to open a jar?

    a. It sucks the lid off.

    b. It twists its body over and over.

    c. It puts its body on the lid.

    d. It throws the jar against the side of a tank.

7. How long does it take an octopus to open the jar?

    a. up to an hour

    b. about a day

    c. a week

    d. a month

8. Which of these is true of an octopus?

    a. It can live outside of water for a long time.

    b. It can take apart an object.

    c. It can take pictures with a camera.

    d. It can learn to count.

9. What happened to the lumpfish?

    a. No one knows.

    b. They crawled out of their tanks.

    c. An octopus ate them.

    d. Scientists ate them.

10. What is the best name for this selection?

    a. Opening Jars

    b. What Scientists Do

    c. A Clever Animal

    d. The Ocean

Remember that each paragraph is indented. A paragraph has a main idea or topic. Most paragraphs have a **topic sentence** that tells what the paragraph is about. The other sentences in the paragraph tell more about the topic.

B **Look back at the selection on pages 75 and 76 to answer these questions.**

1. Count how many paragraphs are in the selection. Write a number, starting with **one**, to the left of each paragraph. How many paragraphs are there?

   _____

2. What are the first and last words of the second paragraph?

   _____   _____

3. Write the last sentence of paragraph three.

   _____

   _____

4. Write the last sentence of paragraph four.

   _____

   _____

5. Write the topic sentence of paragraph seven.

   _____

   _____

   _____

6. Write the topic sentence of paragraph eight.

   _____

   _____

   _____

Name _____ Date _____

C **The topic sentence is missing from each paragraph. Pick the best topic sentence and write it on the lines.**

```
┌─────────────────────────────────────────────────┐
│                  TOPIC BOX                       │
│   An octopus is careful when it looks for a home.│
│   The octopus looks very interesting to us.      │
│   Other animals are also found in the ocean.     │
│   The octopus can be found in almost any ocean.  │
│   The octopus finds many foods in the ocean.     │
└─────────────────────────────────────────────────┘
```

1. _____

_____

_____ An octopus eats crabs and clams. It likes all kinds of shellfish.

2. _____

_____

_____ It finds a home in tiny places in the rocks. It likes to have its home well hidden. If an octopus sees a dark cave, it will move in.

3. _____

_____

_____ Many different kinds of fish live there. They are all different colors and shapes. Animals that need air, such as seals and whales, live there, too.

4. _____

_____

_____ It has a soft body with no bones or shell. Eight long arms and two big eyes stick out from its body. The octopus can even change color to look blue, brown, gray, purple, red, or white.

D Now you are ready to be a writer! Use these topic sentences. Write two more sentences that fit the topic. Write good paragraphs that others will want to read.

Two little children wanted to play with the same toy.

_____

_____

_____

_____

_____

Heavy rain made the ship toss and turn on the water.

_____

_____

_____

_____

_____

E These paragraphs have one or more sentences that do not fit the topic. Make each paragraph better. Draw a line through any sentence that does not fit the topic.

Children need heavy clothes to keep warm when days are cold and icy. Their fingers and toes must be well covered. Children should have thick boots for their feet and heavy gloves for their hands. People like to eat hot soup in the winter. Children also need to wear heavy coats when they go outdoors.

_____

A submarine is a kind of boat that moves under the water. It can move up and down or back and forth near the ocean floor. People eat ham, lettuce, and tomato on their submarine sandwiches. When a submarine is under the water, people in it cannot see to the top of the water. They use special equipment to see what is above the ocean. Plants grow on the ocean floor, too. Submarines can even move under ice in very cold oceans.

Name _____ Date _____

F   **Write each word on the line beside its meaning.**

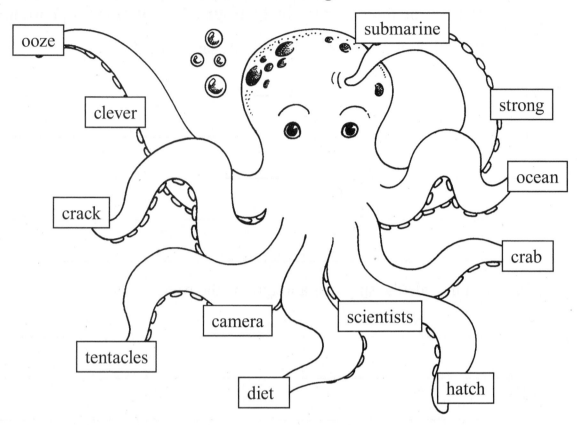

1. a box used to take pictures _____

2. a boat that moves under water _____

3. to slide out slowly _____

4. water where big ships sail _____

5. people who study plant and animal life _____

6. very smart _____

7. sea animal with legs and claws _____

8. long arms on an octopus _____

9. a food plan _____

10. a small space between two things _____

11. come out of an egg _____

12. able to lift heavy things _____

Skills Review: Selections 6–10

A What would you use this equipment for? Write the correct word under each picture of equipment.

schoolwork	basketball	swimming
camping	tennis	ice skating
football	baseball	cooking

1. _____

2. _____

3. _____

4. _____

5. _____

6. _____

7. _____

8. _____

B **Practice! Practice! Practice! The more you practice, the better you are in reading. Choose the correct word to finish each sentence. Write the word on the lines.**

1. The kneepads will (practice, protect, praise) your knee bone if you fall.

   _____

2. The (porcupine, protect, practice) had sharp quills.

   _____

3. Emily was pleased when Mrs. Perkins (practiced, praised, porcupine) her.

   _____

4. Justin always (ready, relaxed, really) by reading funny stories.

   _____

5. Someone who wants to hurt him is his (enemy, equipment, every).

   _____

6. Mark (bounced, brought, boasted) his equipment to the skateboard ramp.

   _____

7. Children who do good work are (stupid, serious, scientist) about doing their homework.

   _____

8. When Ann ran to second (base, bake, back), her friends clapped.

   _____

Name _____ Date _____

C Can you find the phrase that tells who or what the sentence is about? Underline each *who* or *what* phrase.

1. An octopus lived in the crack in the rocks.

2. *Bang, bang* went the beaver's tail.

3. The scientists watched the octopus.

4. "Help!" yelled Sam.

5. Lita came down the tree.

D Now let's find the action phrases. Sometimes only one word is needed to tell the action. Circle the part that tells the action.

1. Emily and Justin laughed.

2. His arm bone was broken.

3. One girl fell in a relay race.

4. The rain fell faster and faster.

5. People skated and practiced.

6. The lizards changed color.

E A *when* phrase tells the time that the action happens. Look at each picture to find out when the action happened. Finish each sentence with one of the *when* phrases in the box.

in the morning	at noon	at night

1. We stayed home _____

_____.

2. Sally rode on a swing _____

_____.

3. Pam woke up _____

_____.

Skills Review: Selections 6–10
Core Skills Reading Comprehension, Grade 3

F Read the selection. In what order did things happen? Draw a line from the question to the right answer.

Mr. Bear had not visited the stream for many months. One evening he was hungry. He remembered that he always got lots of fish at one place in the stream. But this time he found the stream almost dry. There had been no rain for a year. Fish were gone. Mr. Bear had to go to sleep hungry.

1. What came first?   **a.** Fish could not live in the stream any more.

2. What came second?   **b.** No rain fell for a year.

3. What came third?   **c.** Mr. Bear could not find fish.

4. What came fourth?   **d.** Water in the stream got lower.

G Draw a line through any sentence that does not go with the topic sentence of this paragraph.

Bears are always searching for food. Bears eat almost anything they run into. When they come to a stream, they know how to catch as many fish as they want. Bears have white, brown, or black fur. Bears kill and eat any smaller animals they find in the forest. Bears love sweet food. When they find a beehive, they can't wait to eat. They chew up the honey and the bees! Long ago, people used bearskins for rugs.

Selection 11

There was a time when ships had no engines. Large ships that crossed the oceans of the world had only sails to make them go. When the wind did not blow to push the sails, the ships could not move along.

On April 3, 1970, a ship named the *Mary Lee* set sail from the West Indies to Boston. The boat was crowded with twenty-three sailors, the captain, and ten passengers.

Two of the passengers were children named John and Margaret Scott. They were traveling with their parents. John and Margaret always wanted to know how long they had been sailing.

Mr. Scott said, "Cut a thick, deep line on this stick every day at sunset. Then you will know how many days we have been traveling on the ocean."

Traveling was hard in 1769. Some passengers were seasick. Sleeping places were crowded, smelly, and had little air. On the twelfth day of the trip, a sailor named Sam fell into the ocean. Sam had been climbing up the mainsail when he fell off.

Some of the sailors rushed to get ropes to throw to Sam. Sam was splashing in the deep water. Most of the people were watching Sam. Mr. Scott was the first to see the giant fin of a huge fish sticking out of the water.

87

"Danger," yelled Mr. Scott. "Sharks!"

The shark's fin came through the water faster than the boat could travel.

"Hurry with the ropes!" everyone was yelling.

The shark's fin was close to Sam when three ropes hit the water near him. One rope fell almost into Sam's hands. He grabbed it and held on. The sailors pulled hard on the other end of the rope. Sam was almost up to the ship.

But the huge shark leaped out of the water to bite Sam's leg. People looked into the shark's open mouth and saw two rows of sharp teeth.

Just then, Margaret threw the stick at the shark. The shark bit the stick as the sailors pulled Sam up to the deck of the ship. Sam was safe!

Mr. Scott was proud of his children. He let them count the days by making the cuts on the lid of their clothes trunk.

A **Underline the right answer to each question.**

   1. When did this selection take place?

   a. last year

   b. a long time ago

   c. ten months ago

   d. at sunset every day

   2. How many people were on this ship?

   a. twenty-four   **c.** twenty-eight

   b. thirty   **d.** thirty-four

3. How did the ship move through the water?

   a. The ship had a strong engine.

   b. Sailors pulled the ship on ropes.

   c. Wind pushed the sails to make the ship move.

   d. The sails and the engine pushed the ship.

4. Why did John and Margaret cut lines on a stick?

   a. to count the days

   b. to make toys

   c. to tie ropes together

   d. to know what time it was

5. What was this selection mainly about?

   a. how sharks get food

   b. a trip on a sailing ship

   c. how to travel to the West Indies

   d. how to travel on a river

6. How did Sam get back on the ship?

   a. Sailors went to get him in a small boat.

   b. Sailors jumped into the water to get him.

   c. The shark pushed Sam back onto the ship.

   d. Sam held on to a rope and was pulled up.

7. What did the shark want to do with Sam?

   a. use the sailor for food

   b. help Sam back onto the ship

   c. catch the ropes for Sam

   d. make friends with Sam

8. What did <u>not</u> happen to Sam?

   a. He was pulled onto the ship.

   b. He fell into the deep water.

   c. The shark bit him on the leg.

   d. He splashed in the deep water.

9. Where was the ship going?

 a. to the West Indies

 b. to Florida

 c. to Boston

 d. to New York

10. Who was *Mary Lee*?

 a. John Scott's sister

 b. John Scott's mother

 c. a passenger

 d. the ship

11. Which one happened first?

 a. Sam was pulled onto the sailboat.

 b. The shark leaped high out of the water.

 c. The sailors threw ropes to Sam.

 d. People looked into the shark's mouth.

12. What would John and Margaret use today to know the date?

 a. a clock

 b. a stick

 c. a rope

 d. a calendar

13. When did the children cut a deep line on the stick?

 a. every evening

 b. every morning

 c. every week

 d. every hour

14. What is the best title for this selection?

 a. How the Shark Helped Sam

 b. Sailing to the West Indies

 c. A Trip on the Steamboat

 d. A Trip on a Sailing Ship

Name _____ Date _____

B **Can you answer these questions about time?**

1. What was the date when the *Mary Lee* set sail? _____

2. How many years ago was that? To work it out:

   a. Write the number of this year's date. _____

   b. Now write the date of the year when the *Mary Lee* set sail. _____

   c. Take the smaller number from the larger number. Now you know how long ago it was. _____ years

3. In 1869, a steamship called the *American Dragon* sailed from Boston to the West Indies.

   a. How many years ago was that trip? _____

   b. How many years after the *Mary Lee* did the *American Dragon* sail?

   _____ years

C **Choose the right word to write next to the meaning.**

captain	shark	parent	trunk
crowded	traveling	always	seasick
engine	mainsail	passengers	fin

1. _____ machine that makes a car or boat move

2. _____ people who ride on boats, cars, or buses

3. _____ the one who gives orders on a ship

4. _____ a box to hold clothes

5. _____ going from place to place

6. _____ largest sail on a ship

7. _____ part of a fish that helps it move

8. _____ filled with people or things

9. _____ a large fish with sharp teeth

10. _____ a mother or a father

11. _____ every time

D These lists will help you answer the questions. Underline the right answer that tells when something happened.

Times of Day	Longer Times
dawn (sunrise, sunup)	7 days = 1 week
morning	4 weeks = 1 month
noon	12 months = 1 year
afternoon	
evening (sunset, sundown)	
night	
midnight	

1. The passengers could not take baths on the ship. They washed their faces and hands each day just after **sunrise.** When did they wash?

   a. early in the morning

   b. early in the evening

   c. late at night

2. At **dawn**, the sailors woke up and got back to work. When did the sailors wake up?

   a. at sunset

   b. at sunrise

   c. at sundown

3. After **two weeks** on the ship, Mrs. Scott washed some clothes because they had no clean ones left to wear. When did she wash clothes?

   a. after twenty-one days

   b. after seven days

   c. after fourteen days

4. Margaret started making a quilt in **1769**. She finished it in **1771**. How long did it take her to make the quilt?

   a. two months

   b. two years

   c. two weeks

5. Sam the sailor got new boots in **1766**. He was still wearing those boots when he fell in the ocean in **1769**. How old were Sam's boots?

   a. a year old

   b. five years old

   c. three years old

6. They had been traveling on the ship for **three weeks**. They asked the captain how much longer the trip would take. He said, "We should get to Boston in **one more week**." How long will the trip take in all?

   a. about one year

   b. about one month

   c. about one week

7. John and Margaret marked off the days at sea by making a cut on a stick each day at **sunset**. When did they mark the stick?

   a. as the sky was getting light

   b. as the sky was getting dark

   c. at noon when the sun was high in the sky

8. **A year** after they sailed to Boston, Mr. and Mrs. Scott saw some people who had been on the same ship. They talked about the long, hard trip. When did they talk?

   a. twelve weeks after the trip

   b. twelve months after the trip

   c. twelve days after the tip

9. John Scott was born in **1761**. Margaret Scott was born in **1757**.

   a. Which child is older?

   _____

   b. Which one was eight years old when they sailed on the *Mary Lee* in 1769?

   _____

   c. How old was Margaret in 1769?

   _____

E What is a sentence? It is a group of words that has two parts. One part tells who or what the sentence is about. The other part tells the action that the "who" or "what" does.

Each part of a sentence is called a phrase. A phrase does not have both parts of a sentence.

1. What does one sentence part tell?

_____

2. What does the other sentence part tell?

_____

3. What are sentence parts called?

_____

F Read these sentences. Underline the phrase that tells who or what in each sentence. Then circle the action phrase. One is done for you.

1. Fish can swim.

2. The wind blew harder.

3. The ship is turning.

4. Sam fell down.

5. Margaret ran quickly.

G These groups of words look like sentences, but some are not. One phrase is missing in some of them. Put a capital *S* by each one that is a sentence.

_____ 1. Pulled hard on the ropes.

_____ 2. Passengers on the ship were seasick.

_____ 3. Sailor Sam fell off the mainsail.

_____ 4. A big school of fish.

_____ 5. Will get to Boston in one week.

_____ 6. The ship moved slowly.

_____ 7. They made a cut on the stick each day.

Name _____ Date _____

A long time ago, a ship could not leave port until high tide. Low tide means the water is not deep. A ship could get stuck on the sand at the bottom. High tide means the water is much deeper. The ship can float without touching bottom.

On April 3, 1769, the *Mary Lee* was waiting for high tide. The captain and the sailors knew when the tides changed.

The captain watched how deep the water was. He ordered the crew to set sail. Sailors began to climb the ropes. They let out the sails and got them ready. John, Margaret, and the other passengers waved good-bye to their friends.

One sailor stood by the wheel ready to steer the ship. The wind filled the sails and pushed the ship forward. The sailor at the wheel began to steer the ship.

When did these things happen? Write the word *before* or *after* on the line for each phrase.

1. When did the captain order the ship to sail?

   _____ the sailor began to steer

2. When did the crew climb the ropes?

   _____ they let out the sail

3. When did the ship sail?

   _____ the tide was high

4. When did the passengers wave good-bye?

   _____ the ship sailed away

5. When did the *Mary Lee* set sail?

   _____ April 10, 1769

6. When did the sails fill out?

   _____ the captain knew the water was deep enough

I **Read each question. Draw a line to the right answer.**

1. What came first?   **a.** A sailor steered the boat out of the port.

2. What came second?   **b.** Sailors let out the sails.

3. What came third?   **c.** The tide got high.

4. What came last?   **d.** The captain ordered the ship to sail.

J **Use these topic sentences. Write two more sentences that fit each topic. Make good paragraphs that others will want to read.**

Amy found $5.00 on the school playground. _____

_____

_____

_____

Rusty was having a hard time learning to ride the pony. _____

_____

_____

_____

A box fell off the truck when it turned the corner. _____

_____

_____

_____

Selection 12

Several days had passed since Sam, the sailor, was saved from the shark. Then another serious thing happened to the sailing ship. The wind just stopped blowing! With no wind, the *Mary Lee* could not move ahead. It just drifted slowly about. The captain told the sailors to change the sails to catch any light breeze. But no air stirred.

Mrs. Scott said, "Maybe the wind will spring up again when it gets dark."

"I hope so," said John Scott. "It is so hot and still without a breeze blowing."

The sun went down in the west. Darkness crept over the water, but still no wind blew. People began to hope that by dawn a breeze would spring up to send them on their way.

At dawn the sun appeared again, and it began to get light. But still there was no wind. So it went, day after day. No wind blew, and the sails just hung.

Then things became more serious. There was not much water left to drink. The food that should have been enough for the whole trip was running low. The passengers and crew were hot, hungry, tired, and afraid. They could see sharks' fins swimming around the ship.

"Blow, wind!" cried Margaret. "It is strange. At home, I used to hate strong wind because it blew my bonnet off my head!"

97

John said, "Before we got on the ship, I hoped that we would never have storm winds. I was afraid winds would push huge waves over the ship and wash us into the ocean."

Night hours were bad times for the passengers and crew. They were running low on candles. The captain would not let them light the candles after dark. When people could not sleep, they had to sit in the dark and wait for dawn to come.

Each day the sailors put fishing lines over the sides of the ship to catch fish. Often sharks swim over and pulled some of the fish off the hooks.

Just when everyone had almost given up hope, one morning tiny drops of rain began to come down. A light breeze stirred, and the rain fell harder. Then the wind pushed against the sails. Slowly the boat turned and was on its way again.

The captain said, "If the wind keeps blowing, we'll be in Boston in one week." Everyone was happy to hear that.

At sunset, Margaret made one more heavy cut in the lid of the trunk. She showed it to John.

John said, "It seems as if we have been on this ship for years, but it has only been twenty-one days!"

A **Underline the right answer to each question.**

1. What do you think might happen **today** if the wind stopped blowing around a large passenger ship?
   a. People would run low on food and water.
   b. People would have to radio for help.
   c. Helicopters would pull the ship along.
   d. Nothing would happen.

2. How long did people on the *Mary Lee* wait for the wind to blow again?

   a. nine hours   **c.** three years

   b. eight months   **d.** many days

3. How did they know that sharks were nearby?

   a. Fins were sticking out of the water.

   b. They heard the noises of the shark.

   c. Divers saw sharks when they swam under the ship.

   d. Another ship warned them about the sharks.

4. Why did Margaret hate the strong winds on land?

   a. The wind blew her off her feet.

   b. The wind blew her hat off.

   c. The wind made the waves too high.

   d. The wind kept her from traveling.

5. The air <u>stirred</u>. What does this mean?

   a. The air moved.

   b. The wind stood still.

   c. The ship made the wind blow.

   d. They waved a spoon in the air.

6. How did the captain try to get the ship moving?

   a. He told the crew to fix the engines.

   b. He told the crew to change clothes.

   c. He had the sailors row the ship.

   d. He had the sailors change the sails.

7. What was the danger in not sailing on for so long?

   a. The ship could turn over more quickly.

   b. The people got tired of waiting to sail on.

   c. The people did not have enough air.

   d. The people would run out of food and water.

8. Why couldn't they get water to drink from the ocean?

    a. Sharks would not let them get near the water.

    b. Ocean water is not good for drinking.

    c. They might get fish in their mouths from ocean water.

    d. The waves were not high enough.

9. How could they get more food while the ship was still?

    a. from other ships passing by

    b. by growing it in some dirt

    c. by catching fish

    d. by helicopter

10. What can we learn from this selection?

    a. Sharks have a hard time finding food in the ocean.

    b. Ocean travel took a long time on a sailing ship.

    c. People should not travel on ships.

    d. People saw more when they traveled by ship.

11. What do you think might have happened if there had been no strong wind for several months?

    a. The people would have run out of food and water.

    b. The sharks would have eaten the ship.

    c. The sailing ship would have turned over and sunk.

    d. Other ships would have pulled the *Mary Lee* along.

12. What is the best title for this selection?

    a. Saving the Candles

    b. Running Out of Food

    c. How the Wind Blows

    d. A Sailing Ship Without Wind

B **Write the answers to these questions about time.**

1. How many days had the Scotts been on the ship by the end of the selection? _____

2. How many weeks was that? _____

3. They had to travel one more week to reach Boston. How many weeks did the trip take in all? _____

4. When Columbus sailed to the New World, the trip took ten weeks. How many days did that trip take? _____

5. Columbus sailed in 1492. The Scotts sailed in 1769.
   a. Which trip came first? _____
   b. How many years were there between the two trips? _____

C **Which are times of day and which are times of night? Put the right words on the sails of each ship.**

morning	evening	noon	midnight
dawn	darkness	bedtime	sunrise

1.

2.

Day Times

Night Times

101

D Draw lines to match the words and meanings.

1. one week		**a.** name of a month
2. twenty-eight days		**b.** twenty-one days
3. twelve months		**c.** fourteen days
4. three weeks		**d.** four weeks
5. Tuesday		**e.** one year
6. two weeks		**f.** one day of the week
7. August		**g.** a date long ago
8. April 3, 1769		**h.** seven days

E Circle the right answer to each question.

1. John made another cut on the stick each day at **sunset**. When did he do this?

   a. noon   **b.** midnight   **c.** evening   **d.** dawn

2. The storm began at **dawn**. When did the storm start?

   a. early morning   **c.** late evening

   b. early evening   **d.** late afternoon

3. The wind stopped blowing at **sunrise**. When did it stop?

   a. midnight   **b.** dawn   **c.** evening   **d.** noon

4. Sam climbed the ropes to the top of the sails at **noon**. When did he climb the ropes?

   a. as darkness fell   **c.** at sunrise

   b. early morning   **d.** middle of the day

5. They ate fish at **sundown**. When did they eat?

   a. dawn   **c.** late morning

   b. early evening   **d.** middle of the day

6. The ship traveled faster at **night**. When did it go faster?

   a. early morning   **c.** after sunset

   b. before sunset   **d.** at dawn

Name _____ Date _____

F **Are you a careful reader? Did these things happen long ago or do they happen now? Write *long ago* or *now* after each one to tell when it happened.**

1. The Garza family came across the ocean on a huge jet airplane. Two hundred other passengers were on the same plane.

   _____

2. Traveling over land by wagon was a long, dusty trip. The roads were all dirt on dry days and all mud on rainy days. The horses' feet kicked dirt up into people's faces.

   _____

3. When the wind stopped blowing, the big sails just hung. The boat drifted slowly. We had to start the engine to get back to the dock before dark.

   _____

4. They had been riding horses a long time when they came to a fence. Most of the horses jumped over the fence, but Joe's horse stopped. Joe was thrown from the horse. Mary stopped a passing truck and asked the people to call a doctor.

   _____

5. Carmen raced down the hill. She leaned too far and fell off her skateboard.

   _____

6. Will wanted to finish reading his book. But he could not since there was not enough light to see the pages. The candles had burned out. Light from the fireplace was very dim. There was no other way of lighting the house at night.

   _____

7. Jane always had to help Mother at sunrise. First they lit a fire in the large fireplace in the kitchen. Then they hung a pot of water over the fire to get hot. Then they cooked food in the fireplace most of the day.

   _____

G **Find the right word to use in each sentence.**

crew	appeared	breeze	bonnet
always	darkness	drifted	while
serious	several	stirred	enough

1. At dawn, the sun came into sight. Later, it went behind a cloud and then

   _____ again.

2. Just a light wind or _____ would cool us off.

3. What you did is not funny. It is a _____ thing.

4. The wind _____ and moved the leaves a little.

5. Margaret's _____ is tied under her chin.

6. When we walked in the _____, the only light came from
   the moon and stars in the sky.

7. The boat _____ first one way and then the next as the
   wind changed.

8. Since _____ of us are going, we will need six lunches.

9. If there is _____, you will have as much as you need.

10. The ship's _____ was made up of the captain and
    twenty-three sailors.

H **Draw a line from the *who* or *what* phrase to each *action* phrase that makes a good
sentence. Make six different sentences.**

Who or What?

1. The sailors

2. A huge wave

3. Some animals

4. The children

Action

a. have fur.

b. work on ships.

c. splashed over the ship.

d. tied their shoes.

e. live in the water.

Selection 13

Millions of years ago, there were no human beings on earth. There was a time when almost all the world had warm, damp weather. Plants of that time grew quickly and got very large. The animals were also mostly kinds that we do not see today on earth, such as dinosaurs and mammoths. Many of those animals disappeared from the earth long before human beings lived here.

If people had been on the earth to see those strange animals and plants, they would have seen one animal then that we see today. It looks the same now as it did a million years ago. Can you guess which animal it is?

Could it be the lion, the strong king of animals? Is it the swift killer, the tiger? Maybe it is the high-flying eagle? No, it is none of these.

It is the turtle. Scientists have tried for years to find out why dinosaurs and mammoths died, while the slow, creeping turtle is still around. Even in this age, some turtles may live as long as two hundred years. That is something human beings cannot do. Here are some clues that tell why turtles still live on the earth.

Turtles can live almost anywhere. Some spend their lives swimming in the salt water of oceans. Others live in the fresh water of ponds, stream, brooks, swamps, lakes, and even mud holes. Turtles that are taken from their watery homes and placed on land learn to live in the woods and tall grass.

105

Turtles know how to find food easily wherever they happen to live. Ocean turtles eat fish, crabs, clams, shrimp, and snails. Freshwater turtles find tiny fish, snails, insects, water plants, and dead fish. Land turtles eat spiders, roaches, and other insects. They chomp on blueberries, strawberries, mushrooms, worms, and anything else they find.

Turtles have several ways to protect themselves. When in danger, most turtles can pull their heads, tails, and feet into their hard shells. Snapping turtles bite their enemies. Even without teeth, their strong jaws crush and tear. Snapping turtle shells are too small to hide under. Mud turtles never worry about enemies. They smell so bad that other animals will not get close to them.

A **Underline the right answer to each question.**

1. What is the main idea of this selection?

   a. Turtles can easily get away from their enemies by crawling into their hard shells.

   b. Turtles have been around for millions of years because they are not afraid of danger.

   c. Turtles have been around for millions of years because they can live well in many different places.

   d. Turtles have been around for millions of years because they eat only good foods.

2. Which of these belong to a turtle?

   a. four feet, two eyes, strong jaws, a mouth

   b. a hard shell, four feet, two eyes, wings

   c. a long neck, two tiny legs, a strong jaw

   d. a mouth, four short legs, a tail, sharp teeth

3. What was most of the world like when dinosaurs lived?

   a. cold and damp

   b. hot and wet

   c. hot and very dry

   d. cold and dry

4. Where would you find a land turtle?

   a. in a large ocean

   b. in a river or brook

   c. in a swamp or lake

   d. in a forest or garden

5. What is one reason turtles are still on the earth?

   a. They crawl very slowly.

   b. They eat very slowly.

   c. They can protect themselves.

   d. They like living here.

6. What do land turtles eat?

   a. berries and bugs

   b. tiny fish and snails

   c. swamps and mud holes

   d. clams and crabs

7. Which lived on earth first?

   a. human beings

   b. giants and dragons

   c. dogs and cats

   d. dinosaurs

8. Which of these might see an octopus?

   a. a river turtle

   b. a freshwater turtle

   c. a sea turtle

   d. a land turtle

9. Why do some turtles snap at their enemies?

    a. They have no shells.

    b. Their shells are so large that enemies can crawl in.

    c. Their shells are not large enough to protect them.

    d. They are too lazy to go into their shells.

10. How are some turtles like skunks?

    a. They have thick fur.

    b. They protect themselves with a bad smell.

    c. They have thick shells.

    d. They protect themselves by running quickly.

11. What is fresh water?

    a. water that has not been around long

    b. water that comes from the ocean

    c. water that is not salty

    d. water that is not muddy

12. Which one of these sentences is <u>not</u> true?

    a. Some turtles live for two hundred years.

    b. Turtles are protected by hard shells.

    c. Turtles live in many different places.

    d. Turtles chew food with their teeth.

13. What is the best title for this selection?

    a. The People Who Saw Dinosaurs

    b. Millions of Years of Turtles

    c. The Mammoth and the Dinosaur

    d. The Food of the Giant Dinosaur

It is hard to remember all the facts you read. Making an outline of the facts will help you remember them. To make an outline:

1. Write only the main ideas and key facts.

2. Put a number by each main idea and a letter by each fact.

3. Use Roman numerals for the main ideas:

1 = I	3 = III	5 = V	7 = VII	9 = IV
2 = II	4 = IV	6 = VI	8 = VIII	10 = X

Read the selection below.

How Bees Are Like Human Beings

Bees live in groups just as people do. Every bee has a job and must work hard at it. Many bees work together to finish their jobs quickly. Bees that can no longer work are not given food and must die.

Even though bees are fierce fighters, many bees are killed by their enemies. Some ants and bears destroy the hives in search of honey. Dragonflies and skunks eat the worker bees as they fly among the flowers. Bees often become ill from a bee sickness and may die from it.

B **The steps to follow to make an outline are given at the left. After you read a step, finish that part of the outline at the right.**

1. Put the title first.

2. Now find the main topic of the first paragraph. Choose one of these:
   a. Live in hives
   b. Live in groups
   c. Die from no food

   Write it next to Roman numeral I.

3. Choose the main topic of the second paragraph. Write it next to Roman numeral II.
   a. Honey makers
   b. Have many friends
   c. Have many enemies

How Bees Are Like Human Beings

I. _____

  A. _____

  B. _____

II. _____

  A. _____

  B. _____

  C. _____

4. Choose some facts from the first paragraph that fit topic I the best. Choose two facts. Write them next to the letters *A* and *B*.

    a. Work together

    b. Work alone

    c. Have their own jobs

5. Choose facts from the second paragraph that fit topic II the best. Write them next to letters *A, B,* and *C.*

    a. Butterflies

    b. Skunks

    c. Bears

    d. Sickness

    e. Horses

6. Check your outline. It should look like the one below.

How Bees Are Like Human Beings

    I. *Live in groups*

        A. *Work together*

        B. *Have their own jobs*

    II. *Have many enemies*

        A. *Bears*

        B. *Skunks*

        C. *Sickness*

C **How do these animals protect themselves? Draw lines to match these.**

1. eagle	**a.** It hides inside its shell.
2. wasp	**b.** It has a bad smell.
3. goat	**c.** It has sharp quills.
4. skunk	**d.** It has sharp claws.
5. porcupine	**e.** It hides under water.
6. frog	**f.** It has sharp horns.
7. turtle	**g.** It stings its enemies.

D Now you are ready to outline the selection on pages 105 and 106.

1. The title tells you that you will list facts about why turtles have been on the earth for so many years.

2. From these main ideas, choose three. Write them next to Roman numerals I, II, and III.

   a. Eat many things
   b. Move very slowly
   c. Live almost anywhere
   d. Protect themselves

3. Here are the facts to prove the main ideas are true. Write each fact under the right main idea, next to a letter.

   a. Have a bad smell
   b. On land
   c. Dead fish
   d. Insects and berries
   e. In fresh water
   f. Hide in their shells
   g. In salt water
   h. Freshwater plants
   i. Snap at enemies

Why Turtles Have Lived So Long

I. _____

   A. _____

   B. _____

   C. _____

II. _____

   A. _____

   B. _____

   C. _____

III. _____

   A. _____

   B. _____

   C. _____

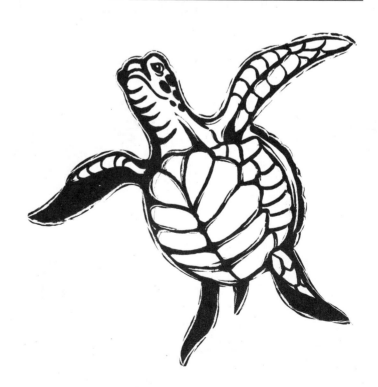

Name _____ Date _____

Choose the right word to write next to the meaning.

crush	damp	protect	swamps
eagle	snap	spend	human beings
swift	enemies	million	

1. wet lands _____

2. many thousands _____

3. those who wish to hurt you _____

4. to save from danger _____

5. people _____

6. a large bird with sharp claws _____

7. to smash _____

8. wet _____

9. very fast _____

10. to bite at quickly _____

Selection 14

One hot summer evening, Rob, Ken, and Angela got tired of playing and went inside their house. As they passed the living room, Rob noticed a beautiful new blue-and-gold box on the table.

"Hey!" yelled Ken. "Maybe this box has candy in it!"

"It's just an empty box," said Angela.

Their mother laughed and said, "Oh no, that box is not empty!"

Angela turned the box over and shook it. Nothing happened.

Rob looked it over carefully. He thought the box might have a secret door. But there was no room for one.

Ken looked over the picture painted on the lid. But it was flat. Nothing was hidden behind it.

Dad and Mom laughed. "You can't see it, but something is in that box!" said Dad.

"We don't believe it!" the three children said.

"Okay!" said their parents.

They took the box to the kitchen sink. Mom filled the sink full of water. Next she took the lid off the box. Then she quickly put the box into the water upside down.

The children were surprised to see little bubbles coming up from the around the box. Their mother had to push hard on the box to keep it down. The children took turns holding the box in the water. They too felt the box trying to come up to the top.

Ken's eyes were big with surprise. "What is pushing and making the bubbles?"

"I know!" shouted Rob. "There is something in the box. You can't see it or smell it or taste it, but you can feel it. It's all around us, and it's in the box, too! It's air!"

"Here is more proof!" said Dad. "Air is in this empty glass."

Dad folded a piece of paper and pushed it into the bottom of the glass. Then he turned the glass upside down in the water in the sink. Again bubbles came up.

Dad had to push hard on the glass to hold it down. Then he pulled it up. When he took the paper out of the wet glass, the paper was dry!

"It must be magic!" whispered Angela.

"No," said Dad. "It's just the air in the glass pushing the water away from the paper."

"I know," said Mom. "Tomorrow let's go to the library and get some books about air. They will show you hundreds of good experiments about air that you can do to surprise your pals."

A **Underline the right answer to each question.**

1. What is the writer of this selection trying to tell us?

    a. how to fool our pals

    b. how to surprise our pals

    b. many ways that air helps us

    d. some facts about air

2. What happened last?

    a. The children peeped into the beautiful box.

    b. Dad did an experiment with paper in a glass.

    c. Mom put the box into the water in the sink.

    d. The children got tired of playing.

3. When we <u>experiment</u>, what do we do?

    a. breathe fresh air

    b. make lots of bubbles

    c. find things in boxes

    d. try things out

4. What happened when Angela shook the box?

    a. Nothing happened.

    b. The lid came off.

    c. It made a loud noise.

    d. Bubbles came out.

5. Why did bubbles form when the glass was put into water?

    a. There was some soap left in the sink.

    b. The paper made bubbles form.

    c. The water was too hot.

    d. Some air got out of the glass and into the water.

6. What do we call air that is moving very fast?

   a. a cloud

   b. a human being

   c. a wind

   d. a living thing

7. Why did Dad have to push down hard on the glass?

   a. The air filled the glass.

   b. He wanted to see if the glass would break.

   c. Dad wanted to break the bubbles.

   d. Dad wanted to know how strong the glass was.

8. Why did Mother say that the box was not empty?

   a. She wanted to tell the children a joke.

   b. She wanted to teach the children.

   c. She made a mistake.

   d. She was telling the children a story.

9. Why is the family going to the library?

   a. for the story hour

   b. to take a walk on a warm day

   c. to find out more about air

   d. to take back some books

10. Why did the paper in the wet glass stay dry?

    a. The air in the glass kept the water out.

    b. The paper in the glass did not let water in.

    c. Dad had put wet paper in the glass.

    d. The bubbles dried the paper.

11. Where do you get your air?

    a. You buy it at the store.

    b. It is everywhere around us.

    c. It comes out of empty boxes.

    d. It comes out of bike tires.

B Air helps to dry things. Air picks up tiny drops of water and carries them away. This is called evaporation. Which sentences below tell about water evaporating in the air? Write the word *evaporation* by the ones you pick.

1. _____ After Rita washed the chalkboard, she saw some parts of it dry. As she watched, more dry spots appeared on the wet board.

2. _____ Angela walked through all the rain puddles. Her shoes were getting wet in the water.

3. _____ Rob hung his socks on the line. The next day, the socks were dry.

4. _____ After the rain, the flowers were wet and hung down. Soon the water disappeared. The flowers lifted up again.

5. _____ Ted blew into a paper bag. The bag got fatter and fatter. Ted hit the bag. It popped with a loud noise as the air came out.

6. _____ Mom put a pitcher full of iced tea on the table. No one drank any because everyone was getting ready to go on a trip. Mom forgot to empty the pitcher. The whole family left. No one came into the house while they were on the trip. When they came back eighteen days later, the pitcher of iced tea was half empty.

C **Before a fire will burn, it must have air. In a small place, a fire can use up all the air. When the air is gone, the fire goes out because it needs more air. These facts can help you answer the questions below. Circle the right answer to each question.**

1. Robert played with matches. Soon his shirt began to burn. Robert yelled, and his whole family ran to help him. What is the best and fastest way to help him?

   a. Give him air.

   b. Give him a drink.

   c. Cover him with a blanket.

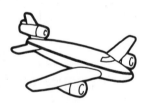

2. Mr. and Mrs. Patel lit a campfire. The wind got stronger and blew sparks all around in the air. They decided to put out the fire. What is the best and fastest way to stop the fire?

   a. Throw dirt on it.

   b. Add more wood.

   c. Run from the fire.

3. The big jet plane made a crash landing at the airport. Quickly the passengers left the plane. But there was still great danger. A fire had started. What is the best and fastest way to stop this kind of fire?

   a. Blow out the flames.

   b. Let the wind blow it out.

   c. Cover the fire.

Name _____ Date _____

D Children at Oaktown School are learning about air. These third graders are going to show the first-grade children some easy experiments to teach them about air. Read what each child wants to show. Then read the experiments. Which experiment will prove what each child wants to show? Match them by writing the letter of the experiment next to the child's face.

AIR IS ALL AROUND US.

AIR CAN MAKE WATER EVAPORATE.

1. _____

2. _____

AIR CAN PUSH.

3. _____

FIRE NEEDS AIR TO BURN.

YOU CAN FEEL AIR, BUT YOU CAN'T SEE IT, TASTE IT, OR SMELL IT.

4. _____

4. _____

Experiments

a.　　　Fill a pan with water. Float a toy sailboat in the water. Blow up a balloon and hold it tightly. Put the balloon opening near the sail. Let the air out slowly. What does the air do to the sailboat?

b.　　　Get a large glass half-filled with soil. Let everyone look at it and touch it. Pour water slowly into the soil. Pour water until it is almost up to the top of the glass. Bubbles will appear. Why?

Name _____ Date _____

c. Make a large fan by folding some strong paper. Fan the air close to the children's faces. What will the children feel?

d. Get two large jars with lids. Take off the lids. Put a candle in each jar lid. Carefully light the candles with a match. Carefully place the jar over one of the candles. Turn the jar in the lid several times to make sure the lid is on tightly. Watch the candles. What happens to the two candles? Why?

e. Get a wet rag. Make four wet spots on the chalkboard. Fan the wet spots with your hands or some paper. What happens? Why?

E **Draw lines to match the words and meanings.**

1. good friends
2. having nothing inside
3. a round body of air
4. a test to find out about something
5. something we don't tell others about
6. facts that show something is true
7. so good that we want to know more about it
8. to put your tongue on something to see what it is

bubble

empty

experiment

believe

interesting

pals

proof

secret

taste

Selection 15

Eddie had lived in a big city all his life. When he was nine, he went to stay all summer with Grandma and Grandpa in the little country village of Oaktown. Eddie was a friendly boy who got to know people easily. Before long, he had many new pals. But sometimes he was unhappy because his friends teased him. There were many things about the country that Eddie did not know yet. Eddie tried to be a good sport when his pals teased him. But inside he was often hurt and angry.

Grandpa said, "If you don't let them see that you mind, they will soon stop teasing you."

Eddie listened to Grandpa. After a few weeks, the other kids got tired of making fun of him. Then Eddie and his friends had many good times together.

One day in August, Eddie was with Bruce and Carol. They were going across a pasture over to the woods. Suddenly, they saw something strange.

"Look! A big piece of land has caved in!" shouted Carol. "It did not look like this yesterday."

They looked into a huge hole and saw a tunnel going under the ground.

"There have been several cave-ins around here in the last two years," said Bruce. "My mom and dad made me promise never to go under the earth to explore them."

Carol said, "My parents also told me never to go into the tunnels underground. They made me promise, too! Anyway, I'm sure nothing is down there."

Eddie yelled, "Well, nobody made me promise anything!"

Bruce and Carol helped Eddie down the hole to the beginning of the tunnel.

"What do you see, Eddie?" asked Carol.

There was no answer from Eddie. Carol and Bruce were angry that they could not explore the underground cave.

"Let's fool Eddie," said Carol. "If he finds something down there, let's tell him that it's hens' teeth."

Bruce laughed and said, "No, Carol, let's say turtles' teeth! Even Eddie would not believe that chickens have teeth!"

Inside the cave, Eddie had found some large dirty things that looked like the bones of a huge animal. In the center of the bones was a long stick covered with dirt. The bones and sticks were too heavy to pull out of the cave. Eddie picked up a few shorter sticks and some small round stones to carry out.

"There's something great down there!" shouted Eddie to the others as he came out. "We should tell the newspaper what we found. We are real explorers!"

Carol and Bruce acted as if they were looking at the stick and stones. They were really trying not to laugh.

When she could keep a straight face, Carol said, "This is an important discovery, Eddie. You have found some turtles' teeth from a huge turtle that lived here millions of years ago. There are no turtles this size living on earth today."

"We should show these to Dr. Grove in town," said Bruce. "She is known all over the world as a scientist. She has discovered bones of animals that lived on earth millions of years ago."

Then the three children ran back through the pasture, over a fence, and down the street to a large green house.

"Eddie, you go in by yourself," said Bruce. "We can't go with you. Dr. Grove might tell our parents that we went underground, too!"

Bruce and Carol hid behind the bushes as Eddie walked up to Dr. Grove's door. Bruce and Carol laughed so hard that they rolled on the ground. Tears ran down their cheeks.

Eddie was scared as he rang the doorbell. A woman came to the door. When Eddie told her about the cave-in, she wanted to know all about it. But when he told her about finding turtles' teeth, she smiled and almost laughed. Eddie began to feel very silly. He had a feeling that his friends might be teasing him again.

But Dr. Grove said, "I would like to see the bigger things you found that you could not carry out. I'll change clothes, and we'll go back there together."

Eddie had an idea of how to get even with the others. He said, "Bruce and Carol, my friends, helped me make this discovery. They were the ones who said that these were turtles' teeth."

"Well, let's take them back with us," said Dr. Grove.

All four of them went back to the cave-in. Carol and Bruce told Dr. Grove about the turtle teeth joke, and they all laughed. But this joke turned out to be more than just fun.

Dr. Grove found out that the big bones in the cave were part of a giant mammoth from millions of years before. The long dirty stick was a spear thrown by a hunter who had killed the mammoth. Dr. Grove said that scientists had not known before that mammoths and people had lived together at the same time in North America.

The three children's names appeared in the newspaper and on TV for their discovery. In the following years, the names of Carol Jenkins, Bruce Wood, Edward Davis, and Oaktown were in science books for having found proof that the first people who lived in our country were here millions of years ago.

A Underline the right answer to each question.

1. What does it mean to try to "keep a straight face"?

   a. to face a straight picture

   b. to keep from laughing

   c. to look straight at someone's face

   d. to draw a picture of a face with straight lines

2. When did Eddie first go down into the tunnel?

   a. the first week he came to Oaktown

   b. before Carol discovered the cave-in

   c. after he went to Dr. Grove's house

   d. after Carol discovered the cave-in

3. Why did Carol say that Eddie had made a big discovery?

   a. She knew that mammoth bones had not been found before.

   b. She was playing a trick on Eddie.

   c. She knew it is hard to find turtles' teeth.

   d. She wanted to make Eddie happy in the country.

4. What new discovery had the children made?

   a. Mammoths had long fur with stripes.

   b. Early people and mammoths lived at the same time.

   c. The right date of the cave-in was January 29.

   d. Mammoths had dug the large hole in the ground.

5. Eddie was a "good sport." What does this mean?

   a. He was a good ball player.

   b. He got into a tunnel without getting hurt.

   c. His picture was on the sports page of the newspaper.

   d. He tried to get along with others.

6. Why was it funny to tell Eddie that the things he found were turtles' teeth?

    a. Turtles' teeth have points on the ends.

    b. Turtles have no teeth.

    c. They were really hens' teeth.

    d. There were no hens and turtles living long ago.

7. What kind of a doctor was Dr. Grove?

    a. a doctor who takes care of pets

    b. a doctor who takes care of people

    c. a scientist who knows about mammoths

    d. a teacher who teaches third graders

8. When was Eddie in Oaktown?

    a. twelve months of the year

    b. June, July, and August

    c. April, May, and June

    d. all of his life

9. How did Grandpa help Eddie make friends?

    a. He yelled at Eddie's pals.

    b. He found the bones.

    c. He caused the cave-in.

    d. He told Eddie not to answer the teasing.

10. What is the best title for this selection?

    a. The Discovery of Turtle Teeth

    b. Dr. Grove, the Explorer

    c. A Great Discovery

    d. A Day in the Pasture

B The main idea tells what is most important about the selection. The title should give you a clue about the main idea. Here are some titles for the selection about Eddie, Carol, and Bruce. Which are good titles for it? Put an *X* by the ones that tell what is important about the selection.

_____ **1.** The Story of the Cave People

_____ **2.** A Great Discovery in Oaktown

_____ **3.** Eddie Listens to Grandpa

_____ **4.** What Mammoths Looked Like

_____ **5.** Exploring Under the Earth

_____ **6.** Carol and Bruce Play a Joke

C Many less important facts are in a selection to help you learn about the main ideas. These less important facts are called details. Can you match the details to the people? Some details match more than one person. Use the numbers *1, 2, 3,* and *4* for the people's names.

1. Eddie Davis

2. Dr. Joan Grove

3. Carol Jenkins

4. Bruce Wood

_____ **a.** lives in North America

_____ **b.** is a female human being

_____ **c.** lives in a big city

_____ **d.** is a child

_____ **e.** is a male human being

_____ **f.** is a scientist

_____ **g.** visits grandparents

_____ **h.** lives in a village

_____ **j.** keeps promises to parents

_____ **k.** does not like to be teased

Name _____ Date _____

D Scientists have found bones of dead animals that lived millions of years ago. People were not living on earth back then. Scientists have learned enough about these animals to tell what they looked like. Read the details of each discovery. Which scientist worked on it? Write the scientist's name under the picture of the animal he or she studied.

1. _____   3. _____   5. _____

2. _____   4. _____   6. _____

a.   Dr. Morgan found bones of a strange animal in the side of a hill. The animal had been the size of foxes we see today. It had four long, thin legs. It had hard hooves for feet. Dr. Morgan said this animal was a very early kind of horse.

b.   Dr. Yee found eggs of strange animals in the rocky earth. These animals were any size from tiny to huge. Their two back feet were claws. Dr. Yee thinks they were very early kinds of birds because on their front claws were large pieces of skin like wings.

c.   Dr. Stern studied these strange animals in many parts of the world. These huge animals were covered with thick hair and walked on four thick legs. Dr. Stern thinks they were early elephants because they had long tusks or horns on their faces. They ate grass and other plants.

d. Dr. Garza found the teeth of a strange kind of lizard that lived billions of years ago. These large lizards walked on four very short legs. They had long tails that dragged on the ground behind them. They had big pieces of skin and bone on their backs that stood up like huge sails. They killed other lizards for food with their sharp teeth and claws.

e. Dr. Grove became well known for studying huge lizards that lived near water. They walked on two long, strong back legs. They had short, webbed front feet and were good swimmers. Each had a nose and mouth shaped like a duck's bill.

f. Dr. Serra found the body of this animal frozen in a huge block of ice near the South Pole. This animal looked very much like dinosaurs that ate plants. It had a huge body, a long, thin neck, and a tiny head. But in place of legs it had four flippers. Dr. Serra knew that this animal had lived in the water swimming and eating fish.

E **Draw lines to match the words and meanings.**

1. something you found
2. a very tiny town
3. made fun of someone
4. a tool for hunters
5. heard what was said
6. the day before today
7. a long hole under the ground
8. to search in strange places
9. said you would do something
10. a place where the earth sinks
11. grassy land where cattle eat
12. an animal that crawls on its four short legs
13. something that rings

teased

pasture

explore

yesterday

discovery

important

tunnel

cave-in

spear

lizard

village

doorbell

listened

promised

Selection 16

Ranger Smith said, "There has been little rain this year. The trees and grass are very dry."

"Yes, everyone must be more careful in the woods now," said Ranger Reed. "After you finish with your campfire, put it out."

"Put water on the fire first," said Ranger Smith. "Stamp on it and then put sand on it. Push the wood around."

"Never leave a fire until all the sparks are put out," said Ranger Reed.

Then the rangers told us about two different families.

Ranger Smith said, "The Peach family was camping out in the woods in June. They slept each night in sleeping bags in their tents. On their last morning here, they cooked breakfast over a fire."

"Then they packed all their things. Mrs. Peach put water on their fire to put it out. Mr. Peach stamped on it. They waited until no fire was left. Then the Peach family got into their car."

Then Ranger Reed said, "The Stone family was in the woods, too. They were not careful. They made a campfire. When they were ready to leave, they did not put water on the fire. They just left the fire burning. They got in their car and went on down the road."

A **Underline the right answer.**

1. What do you think the Peach family will do next?

   a. They will run the car over the fire.

   b. They will drive away.

   c. They will call the firefighters.

   d. They will build a new fire.

2. Where do you think the Peach family will go next?

   a. home

   b. back into the tent

   c. to visit a neighbor

   d. to ask the park ranger how to put out a fire

3. What did the Peach family cook over the fire on the last day?

    a. dinner

    b. supper

    c. breakfast

    d. a snack

4. When did the Peach family go camping?

    a. July

    b. June

    c. August

    d. May

5. Why do you think the Peach family used tents?

    a. to keep the fire burning

    b. to keep warm and dry

    c. to stop the fire from burning

    d. to hide from the park ranger

6. Which do you think will most likely happen after the Stone family leaves?

    a. They family will get a new car.

    b. Their car will catch fire.

    c. The rain will put the fire out fast.

    d. The fire will keep burning.

7. Why is it a bad idea to leave a fire burning?

    a. The food will not be good.

    b. The woods may catch on fire.

    c. The next campers won't want your fire.

    d. It will make the other campers too hot.

8. What is a good title for this selection?

    a. How to Put Out Fires

    b. How to Be a Ranger

    c. How to Build a Fire

    d. How to Set Up a Tent

B Choose the right word to write beside the meaning.

burning	finish	sparks
camping	ranger	stamp
careful	slept	tent

1. someone whose job is taking care of the woods _____

2. on fire _____

3. to hit your feet down on something _____

4. sleeping and eating in the woods _____

5. come to the end _____

6. small bits of fire _____

7. a place to sleep outdoors _____

8. trying to be safe _____

C Read the selection below. Find the safe way out of the picnic grounds.

The town of Butterfield was having its Fourth of July picnic. Many people were there when a fire started. Very quickly, fire was all around the picnic grounds. Five roads went out of the picnic grounds. Four roads were not safe because the fire had reached them. Only one safe way was left.

The firefighters told people to go out this way. People who listened were safe. Can you get out by doing what the firefighters said to do? Draw a line on the map on page 132 to show the safe way out of the picnic grounds.

1. First, take the road that goes under the bridge.

2. Next, go past the outdoor cooking grills.

3. Then, go by the big flower garden.

4. Then, go past the swimming pool to the playground.

5. Go through the playground to the ball field.

6. Go by the ball field.

7. Now you must go across the brook to a big white house. The fire cannot reach here. You are safe!

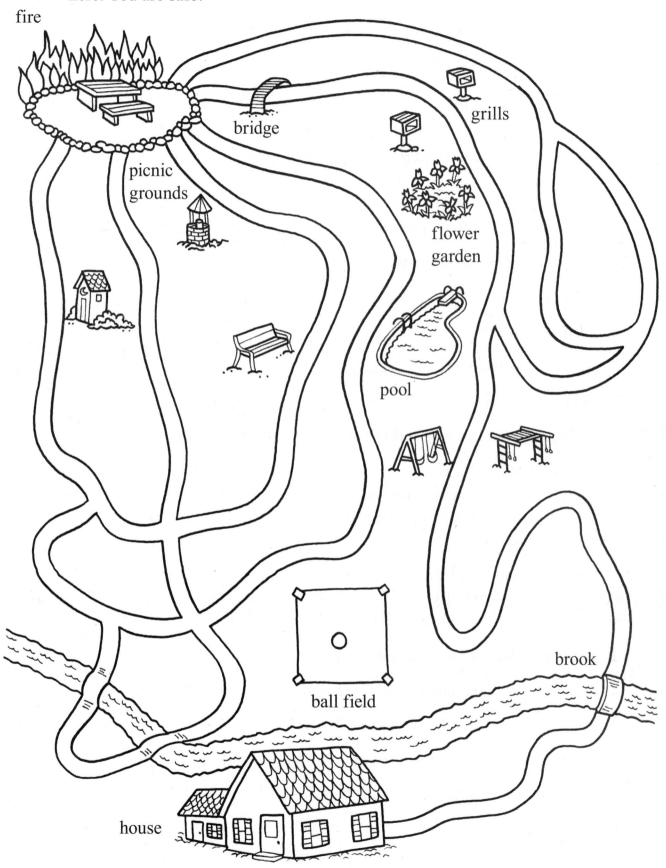

fire

picnic
grounds

bridge

grills

flower
garden

pool

brook

ball field

house

D **Are you careful to do things the safe way? Read each pair of sentences. Put *S* by sentences that tell a safe way. Put *NS* by ways that are not safe.**

_____ 1. If the light is red, hurry across the street on your bike.

_____ 2. If the light is red, wait for a green light before you go across on your bike.

_____ 3. Don't run in the halls at school. You might fall or run into someone.

_____ 4. Run in the halls, and you will get to your classroom faster.

_____ 5. Never put toys on steps. Someone might fall on them.

_____ 6. Put toys on the bottom step.

_____ 7. The best way to learn to swim is to jump into deep water. The water will hold you up.

_____ 8. Don't go into deep water if you cannot swim. Have someone with you when you swim.

_____ 9. When you ride in a car, don't put your arm too far out of the window.

_____ 10. Never put your arms out of car or bus windows.

_____ 11. When the fire bell rings, get in line as fast as you can. But clean your desk off first.

_____ 12. When the fire bell rings, walk into line as fast as you can. Look at the teacher and do what you are told.

_____ 13. If a bee comes near you, hit it fast with a book.

_____ 14. If a bee comes near you, stand still. Don't move fast. The bee will go away.

E **Read the sentences. What do you think will happen next? Circle the right sentence.**

1. A girl is playing soccer. She kicks her ball onto a busy street. She runs in front of a car to get her ball.

   a. The car might hit her.

   b. She will win the race.

   c. A dog will run after the car.

2. Some people start a fire. They leave and go home. The fire grows. Some deer and a squirrel see the fire.

   a. The animals will help put out the fire.

   b. The fire will get bigger.

   c. The campers will put out the fire.

3. A boy wants to roller skate. He puts on his skates inside his home. He skates down the stairs outside his door.

   a. He will fall and get hurt.

   b. He will get clean this way.

   c. He will get on a bus.

4. A woman is driving. She notices she has a flat tire. She pulls over to a safe place. She gets out the equipment she needs.

   a. She will call the firefighters.

   b. She will change the tire.

   c. She will get a new car.

5. A man is moving his wet clothes from the washing machine to the dryer.

   a. The clothes will get burned.

   b. He will put on the wet clothes.

   c. The clothes will get dry.

6. A woman walks into her bedroom. She notices that there is water dripping from the ceiling. There is a hole in the ceiling.

   a. She will take a bath.

   b. Her clothes will be washed.

   c. She will find a bucket to catch the water.

Selection 17

On Tuesday, some of Daisy's classmates asked, "Did you bring your check?"

"What check?" asked Daisy.

It was time to get back to work. No one had time to answer Daisy.

On the way home that afternoon, Daisy met her friend Tom. Tom lived next door to her. Daisy began to cry as she told Tom she needed a check.

"What kind of check?" asked Tom.

Daisy whispered, "I don't know. I didn't understand."

"Let's try this check," said Tom. He gave Daisy a piece of pink paper. He made a big √ on it.

On Wednesday morning, Daisy was happy when she gave the teacher the check. Mrs. Boone was <u>not</u> happy!

On the way home, Daisy met Tom again.

"Let's see what kind of check Mrs. Boone wants," Tom said. "We know it's not a check like the one on the pink paper. Do you think it is a check like the ones on my cap? Or, can it be some checkers?

Daisy didn't know, so they went to ask Mrs. Boone.

Mrs. Boone looked surprised. "Daisy, you need a check to pay for the trip to see the pandas," she said.

"Now we understand!" said Tom. "When we talk about checks, we must know what kind of check is needed."

This is the check Daisy's mom gave her.

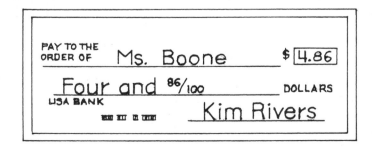

PAY TO THE
ORDER OF   Ms. Boone $ 4.86
          Four and ⁸⁶/₁₀₀   DOLLARS
USA BANK
                    Kim Rivers

A Underline the right answer to each question.

1. Why did Daisy cry?

   a. She had too many checks.

   b. She lost her check.

   c. She didn't have a check.

   d. She got the wrong check.

2. What is this selection about?

   a. a girl who did not see the pandas

   b. a girl who lost something

   c. a girl who didn't understand

   d. a girl who played a trick

3. Why did Daisy need help?

   a. Her mother did not have any checks.

   b. She did not know what kind of check to get.

   c. She always tripped.

   d. She didn't have any friends

4. Who was trying to help Daisy?

   a. a girl in her class   **c.** her mother

   b. a boy in her class   **d.** her neighbor

5. What happened first?

   a. Daisy's check on pink paper

   b. the trip to see the pandas

   c. the check Daisy's mother gave her

   d. Mrs. Boone looking surprised

6. Why did the class need the checks?

   a. to see if their work was good

   b. to pay for a trip to the zoo

   c. to get new caps

   d. to play checkers

7. What did Tom and Daisy learn?

    a. Words must be spelled right.

    b. They must learn a new language.

    c. A word can have many meanings.

    d. It is important to be polite.

8. What surprised Mrs. Boone about Daisy?

    a. Daisy knew Tom.

    b. Daisy did not know about the check.

    c. Daisy had checks on her coat.

    d. Daisy did not want to see the pandas.

B **Words can have many meanings. Draw a line from the picture to the correct sentence.**

1.

    a. He checked the children's work.

2.

    b. She has a checked blanket.

3.

    c. He checks his work on the computer.

4.

    d. They play checkers.

5.

    e. She pays with a check.

C If you read carefully, you can tell who wrote these letters. Write the name from the box under the letter.

Mrs. Boone	Pam Panda
Tom	Daisy

1.   Dear Mrs. Rivers,

As you know, I live next door. Last week, I met Daisy after school. She needed help again. She couldn't find her homework. I told her to think about all of the places she had been that day. She did find her homework that day.

Yours,

_____

2.   Dear Mrs. Rivers,

Daisy has been working very hard. She did very well on her math test. She told the class all about pandas when we went to the zoo. The class learned a lot from her.

I hope Daisy keeps up the good work.

Yours,

_____

3.   Dear Mr. Zookeeper,

Why are all these people looking at us? They talk to us. They tap on the windows. They will not let us sleep. If this keeps up, we will hide every day during visiting hours.

Yours,

_____

D **Circle the letter of the right meaning for each underlined word or words.**

1. Daisy's <u>classmates</u> knew about the trip.

   a. brothers and sisters

   b. the children in her room at school

   c. the children in the city

2. Daisy was afraid that she would <u>trip</u>.

   a. go away

   b. forget

   c. fall

3. The class <u>took a trip</u>.

   a. fell down

   b. checked their work

   c. went somewhere

4. Daisy <u>forgot</u> her lunch.

   a. took it home

   b. ate all of it

   c. did not remember to bring it

5. Daisy <u>understood</u> what she needed.

   a. knew   **b.** liked   **c.** cared about

6. "Did you bring your check?" <u>questioned</u> the teacher.

   a. asked

   b. answered

   c. laughed

E **Circle the best title for each selection.**

1.   One evening, a man came to the door. He had long whiskers, and he talked funny. The children were afraid of him. They did not let him into the house. The man laughed and took off the whiskers. It was only Uncle Billy trying to be funny.

   a. The Funny Whiskers

   b. The Funny Whispers

   c. The Sad Woman

2.   Our teacher, Miss Blue, always knows what we are doing. She seems to know what we are thinking, too! One day, I was mad at Tommy. I didn't tell anyone, but Miss Blue knew. She said, "Stay after school and help me. That will be better than fighting."

  a. Miss Blue Forgets Something

  b. Tommy Stops a Flight

  c. How Did She Know?

3.   Sue was at the pond. A big bee buzzed around her. She ran away. The bee flew after her and swooped down onto Sue's nose. Sue stood very still. She was afraid.

  a. A New Friend

  b. A Bee Lands on a Flower

  c. A Bee Lands on a Nose

F **If you understand all the words in a sentence, you will know what the sentence means. Underline the sentence that has the closest meaning to the first one.**

1. The child gave the teacher a check.

  a. The child gave the teacher flowers.

  b. The child gave the teacher money.

  c. The child gave the teacher nothing.

2. Daisy and her class took a trip.

  a. They went away.

  b. They fell down.

  c. Daisy fell down.

3. Daisy followed her friends.

  a. She walked after them.

  b. She walked before them.

  c. She went the other way.

Name _____ Date _____

Skills Review: Selections 11–17

A After you read the selection, write the people's names under the houses where
they live. Find their names in the selection.

Detective Donna Strikes Again

At eleven o'clock, Mother said to Donna, "Will you please go to get your brother Nicky?
He has to go to see the doctor at twelve o'clock. He is at Scott's house."

Donna and Mother knew that Scott lived at the end of Dean Road. But they did not
know the number of Scott's house. They could not get Scott's phone number because they
did not remember Scott's last name. But Donna was sure she would find the right house.

She went to Dean Street and looked at the five houses at the end.

_____ _____ _____ _____ _____

She knew that the last house must belong to Mary Burns because Nicky had gone to her
house before to swim. Donna could tell that the first house was the home of Nicky's friends
Jane and Jessie Horn, the best baseball players in the neighborhood.

When she looked at the middle house, she knew that it was the home of Gus West. Gus
always spent Saturday and Sunday working in the large gardens around the house.

Nicky had told Donna that Scott lived next door to Gus. On which side of the Gus did
Scott live? Donna thought again. She remembered hearing that Mr. Pepper never let
children play around the wooden deer in his yard. He always chased children away.

Now Donna knew which house was Scott's. She rang the doorbell and found Nicky and
Scott inside.

B **Answer these questions about the selection? Find each answer at the right. Write it under the question.**

1. Where was Nicky?

   _____

   _____

2. When did Mother tell Donna to go find her brother?

   _____

3. How did Donna find Nicky?

   _____

4. Why did Mother want Nicky?

   _____

   _____

5. How did Donna know that the first house was not Scott's?

   _____

   _____

6. Where was the swimming pool?

   _____

7. Where was the wooden deer?

   _____

8. Who lives in the first house?

   _____

a. at eleven o'clock

b. to take him to the doctor

c. around the middle house

d. by thinking

e. because of the baseball diamond

f. Mary Burns

g. by using the phone book

h. at a friend's house

i. at twelve o'clock

j. Jane and Jessie Horn

k. at the first house

l. at the fourth house

m. at the last house

Name _____ Date _____

C This table of contents comes from a book called *Ways of Travel*. Underline the right answers to the questions about it.

<table>
<tr><td colspan="2">**Table of Contents**</td><td>PAGE</td></tr>
<tr><td colspan="2">I. Travel in Early Times . . . .</td><td>5</td></tr>
<tr><td></td><td>Chapter 1 Travel on Foot. . . . .</td><td>9</td></tr>
<tr><td></td><td>Chapter 2 Rowboats and Sailboats . . . .</td><td>15</td></tr>
<tr><td></td><td>Chapter 3 Wagons and Coaches . . . .</td><td>18</td></tr>
<tr><td></td><td>Chapter 4 Travel on Animals. . . . .</td><td>24</td></tr>
<tr><td colspan="2">II. Travel Today . . . .</td><td>31</td></tr>
<tr><td></td><td>Chapter 5 Travel on Land . . . .</td><td>38</td></tr>
<tr><td></td><td>Chapter 6 Travel on the Seas. . . . .</td><td>38</td></tr>
<tr><td></td><td>Chapter 7 Air Travel . . . .</td><td>53</td></tr>
<tr><td></td><td>Chapter 8 Travel Underground . . . .</td><td>59</td></tr>
</table>

1. What do you think this book is about?

   a. different kinds of people

   b. how people get from place to place

   c. how scientists help us travel

2. In which chapter would you read about helicopters?

   a. Chapter 4   **b.** Chapter 5   **c.** Chapter 7

3. Which of these might you find in Chapter 6?

   a. a sailboat   **b.** a coach   **c.** a jet plane

4. What is the first part of the book about?

   a. how people travel now

   b. how people will travel

   c. how people traveled long ago

5. Which of these might you find in Chapter 4?

   a. travel in a submarine

   b. travel on a sailing ship

   c. travel on a horse

6. What might be found on page 22?

    a. riding on camels and horses

    b. riding on trains

    c. riding in a coach

7. What can we be sure of about this book?

    a. It has only two chapters.

    b. It is about things that are true.

    c. It is about make-believe things.

8. What might be found on page 56?

    a. traveling underground

    b. travel by planes or helicopters

    c. air travel and the cave people

D   **What is the main idea of each paragraph below? Look in the box. Then write the main idea under the paragraph.**

the daytime sky	equipment for school
how travel began	the cookbook

All children must bring three pencils to school. They may bring their own paper and a ruler, too.

1. _____

At first, people went places by walking on land. Then they found that they could sit on logs and travel over water, too.

2. _____

Kim picked the book she liked best. It had a picture of food on the cover. Inside were many ways to cook foods.

3. _____

Name _____ Date _____

E Look for the main idea of each paragraph below.

Wind, Our Friend and Enemy

A strong wind can help human beings. It can quickly dry wet clothes that hang on the line. After rain has fallen, the wind evaporates water that stays on sidewalks and roads. Wind pushes and turns windmills that pump water. Wind pushes against sails of boats and sends them on their way. Wind can be fun for people when it pushes kites and balloons about in the sky.

The strong wind can be bad for human beings, too. It can blow rain and snow into people's faces. Then people cannot see where they are walking. It blows rain and snow about on roads, too. Then drivers may run into things with their cars. Storm winds can blow down trees and signs. Very strong winds even break windows and blow roofs off buildings.

Choose the main idea of each paragraph from this box.

> Wind can hurt people.
> Wind is air that moves fast.
> People can make air move.
> Wind can help people.

1. Write the main idea of the first paragraph here.

_____

_____

2. Write the main idea of the second paragraph here.

_____

_____

F **Read the selection. Then answer the questions.**

Flying High

"My bonnet!" yelled Margaret. She stopped in the middle of the street. Her hands grabbed her head, but the bonnet was gone!

Margaret had left the ribbons on her hat untied. The breeze sailed it down the street. Margaret ran after the hat. The wind was too fast.

A dog ran after it, but he could not reach it. Some men raced for it. But it was too late! The wind changed direction, and the bonnet landed on the roof of a building.

When did these things happen? Write the word *before* or *after* on the line for each phrase.

1. When did the wind change direction?

   _____ the dog ran after the bonnet

2. When did Margaret grab her head?

   _____ the bonnet was gone

3. When had Margaret left the ribbons untied?

   _____ the wind sailed the bonnet away

4. When did men race to get the bonnet?

   _____ the dog ran to get it

5. When did the wind change direction?

   _____ the bonnet landed on the roof

6. Which one fits the end of the selection? Circle it.

   The hat fell in the mud.

   A horse stepped on the hat.

   The hat was in a high place.

   A man put on the hat.

Answer Key

A
1. a
2. b
3. b
4. a
5. b
6. c
7. b
8. c

B
1. Ann
2. Mack
3. Mack
4. Joe
5. Kate
6. Kate
7. Beth
8. Ted
9. Joe
10. Sandy
11. Della

C
1. chipmunk
2. whispered
3. resting
4. thinner
5. cheek
6. stripes
7. tired
8. oldest
9. strange

D
2. no error
3. the"
4. Oh!"

E
1. "Tomorrow . . . party," —Joe
2. "I'm . . . birthday."—Mack
3. "I'm . . . now," / "Come . . . me." —Joe
4. no one
5. "This . . . Bob." —Joe
6. "I'll . . . farm," / "because . . . bugs." —Mack
7. "But . . . house," —Joe
8. "Bob . . . things," / "I'll . . . together." —Mack

F
1. His cheeks were full of seeds.
2. He took the seeds to his home in the ground.
3. He cannot find much food in the winter.
4. She flies south to warmer places.
5. His mouth was full of seeds.

6. Scene two
7. Animals are talking to each other like people do.
8. d

Selection 2: Paired
pages 7–11

A
1. c
2. b
3. c
4. c
5. a
6. b
7. b
8. a

B
1. a
2. b

C
1. b
2. c
3. a
4. a

Selection 3: Paired
pages 12–18

A
1. a
2. b
3. c
4. c
5. c
6. b
7. a
8. c
9. a
10. c

B
1. explorer
2. decision
3. difficult
4. canoes
5. discoveries
6. governor
7. wilderness
8. store

C Make sure students use details from the selection to tell why Lewis and Clark are or are not heroes.

D
2. ONE
3. ONE
4. BOTH
5. ONE
6. BOTH
7. ONE
8. BOTH
9. ONE
10. ONE
11. BOTH
12. BOTH

E
1. b
2. c
3. a
4. b
5. a

Selection 4
pages 19–24

A
1. b
2. a
3. c
4. c
5. b
6. b
7. b
8. c
9. b
10. b

B Stanza 1: e, Stanza 2: a, Stanza 3: d, Stanza 4: b, Stanza 5: c

C
1. respect
2. neighborhood
3. gazed
4. mirror
5. climbed
6. promised
7. sparkles
8. ladder

D
1. father
2. poet
3. sister
4. father
5. mother
6. poet and sister
7. father and mother

E Children should give reasons why they would or would not want their own treehouse.

F
1. Building a treehouse
2. Part 1
3. a. page 19
   b. page 36
   c. page 48
   d. page 56
   e. page 26

Selection 5
pages 25–30

A
1. b	5. c
2. c	6. a
3. a	7. c
4. b	

B
1. eagle
2. c
3. a

C
1. Ralph and Ellen were working on a puzzle.
2. They had worked on the puzzle for two weeks.
3. They went out of the room to ask Mom to look at the picture.
4. Mom will help Ralph and Ellen put the puzzle back together.
5. Answers will vary.

D
1. sweeps
2. cleaned
3. club
4. joke
5. save
6. cracked

Skills Review: Selections 1–5
pages 31–36

A
1. nests
2. farm, rocks, trees, ground
3. **a.** 39   **b.** 14   **c.** 21
   d. 41, 54   **e.** 11   **f.** 7
4. c

B
1. a	3. b
2. c	4. a

C
1. doll
2. b
3. c

D
1. guide
2. governor
3. canoe
4. cheek
5. difficult
6. discovery
7. doubled
8. tired
9. gather
10. stripes

E
1. Lewis
2. Clark
3. Lewis
4. Jefferson

F
1. wilderness
2. Their parents won't let them. It's too cold.
3. from her brother Lou
4. in the living room
5. the wilderness
6. Scene 1
7. Answers should be supported with a reason.
8. b
9. b
10. a

Selection 6
pages 37–46

A
1. b	8. d
2. d	9. d
3. b	10. c
4. a	11. c
5. d	12. a
6. a	13. b
7. c	

B
1. equipment
2. head
3. champion
4. practicing
5. hours
6. better
7. awful
8. boast
9. rack
10. bones
11. elbow, knee
12. busy
13. stones, hurt
14. elbows

C
1. On the Ramp 60
2. What You Must Wear 22
3. Safe Places for Practice 51
4. Tricks on the Skateboard 80

D
1. Styles of Skateboarding 74
2. Safety Tips 31
3. Care of a Skateboard 10
4. Safe Places for Practice 51

E
1. Dictionary
2. Dictionary
3. Table of Contents
4. Dictionary
5. Table of Contents

F Answers will vary.

G
1. Mom
2. Mark
3. Julia
4. Eric
5. Dad
6. Answers will vary. Students should write their opinion about an event in the story. They should write their own name on the line.

Selection 7
pages 47–56

A
1. d	4. c
2. a	5. d
3. d	6. b

B
1. relay	5. usually
2. serious	6. muscles
3. praise	7. clumsy
4. relax	8. bounce

C
1. underline *Justin*; circle *can practice*
2. underline *Emily*; circle *shouted*
3. underline *the basketball*; circle *Up, up went*

D
1. at night
2. in the afternoon
3. in the morning

E
1. on the mat
2. on the first floor

F
1. Emily and Justin
took swimming lessons
Garza Middle School
Every Thursday and Friday
2. Emily
learned to dive
into the pool
during her second lesson
3. Justin
does sit-ups
in his bedroom
Every morning

4. Justin's parents
   took many pictures
   on the playground
   the last day of school

G 1. to see better
   2. to have fun
   3. to protect her head
   4. to hear better

H 1. with her tongue
   2. with two sticks
   3. in a pool

I 1. in the spring
   many birds
   all over the world
   kill insects
   for food
   In the spring, many birds all
   over the world kill insects for
   food.
   2. every morning
   many children
   travel
   across town
   by car and bus
   to reach the school
   Every morning, many
   children travel across town
   by car and bus to reach the
   school.

J 1. to become less clumsy
   2. in the water
   3. twice a week
   4. by doing sit-ups
   5. to get better at sports
   6. twice a day

Selection 8: Paired
pages 57–64

A 1. c   7. d
   2. b   8. c
   3. d   9. d
   4. c   10. b
   5. c   11. b
   6. b   12. d

B 1. brought
   2. capture
   3. taste
   4. hooves
   5. protect
   6. gobbled
   7. strange
   8. beak
   9. beautiful
   10. enemies

C 1. 20   3. 3
   2. Most   4. 6

D 1. unlocked
   2. unloved
   3. unanswered
   4. unchanged
   5. unkind
   6. unafraid
   7. uneaten
   8. unseen
   9. unread

E 1. c   3. c
   2. b

F 1. Owls are the greatest mouse
   and rat hunters in the world.
   2. Goats are interesting, funny
   animals.

G Answers will vary.

Selection 9: Paired
pages 65–72

A 1. b   7. b
   2. d   8. c
   3. a   9. c
   4. b   10. d
   5. d   11. a
   6. d

B 1. dam
   2. dare
   3. begged
   4. quills
   5. bragged
   6. scarlet
   7. anger
   8. touch

C Write *un* before each word.
   1. e   4. d
   2. c   5. b
   3. a

D 1. b
   2. Answers will vary. Possible
   answers:
   a. Lita is a lizard.
   b. Lita talks to the other
   animals.
   c. Lita is afraid.

E 2. The tree shakes a little
   3. The beaver warns the others.
   4. Other beavers get out of
   the way.
   5. The beaver takes the last bite.
   6. The tree falls.

F 2. after
   3. before
   4. before
   5. after

G 2. g   5. f
   3. a   6. b
   4. d   7. e

H 2. same   7. different
   3. different   8. same
   4. different   9. different
   5. different   10. same
   6. same

I Selection 8: c. The theme is
   learning you do not need the
   change.; d. Lita learns that some
   animals have horns.; i. Lita talks
   to a goat.
   Both Selections: a. The selection
   takes place in a forest.; f. The
   characters are all animals.; g. All
   the animals speak.
   Selection 9: b. The theme is
   learning you do not need to
   change.; e. Lita learns that she
   is beautiful.; h. Lita meets a
   porcupine.

149

Selection 10
pages 75–82

A 1. a   6. c
    2. d   7. a
    3. c   8. b
    4. b   9. c
    5. d   10. c

B 1. eight
    2. Most, best
    3. It can ooze out of the crack when it wants to get food or swim.
    4. Others go back to the bottom of the ocean.
    5. Scientists can teach an octopus to open jars.
    6. An octopus in a tank will often cause trouble.

C 1. The octopus finds many foods in the ocean.
    2. An octopus is careful when it looks for a home.
    3. Other animals are also found in the ocean.
    4. The octopus looks very interesting to us.

D Answers will vary. Students' sentences should support the topic sentence.

E First paragraph: People like to eat hot soup in the winter. Second paragraph: People eat ham, lettuce, and tomato on their submarine sandwiches. Plants grow on the ocean floor, too.

F 1. camera   7. crab
    2. submarine   8. tentacles
    3. ooze   9. diet
    4. ocean   10. crack
    5. scientists   11. hatch
    6. clever   12. strong

Skills Review: Selections 6–10
pages 83–86

A 1. camping   5. swimming
    2. ice skating   6. cooking
    3. schoolwork   7. basketball
    4. baseball   8. tennis

B 1. protect   5. enemy
    2. porcupine   6. brought
    3. praised   7. serious
    4. relaxed   8. base

C 1. An octopus
    2. the beaver's tail
    3. The scientists
    4. Sam
    5. Lita

D 1. laughed
    2. was broken
    3. fell
    4. came
    5. skated and practiced
    6. changed

E 1. at night
    2. at noon
    3. in the morning

F 1. b   3. a
    2. d   4. c

G Bears have white, brown, or black fur. Long ago, people used bearskins for rugs.

Selection 11
pages 87–96

A 1. b   8. c
    2. d   9. c
    3. c   10. d
    4. a   11. c
    5. b   12. d
    6. d   13. a
    7. a   14. d

B 1. April 3, 1769
    2. a. (this year's date)
      b. 1769
      c. (difference between this year and 1769)
    3. a. (difference between this year and 1869)
      b. 100

C 1. engine
    2. passengers
    3. captain
    4. trunk
    5. traveling
    6. mainsail
    7. fin
    8. crowded
    9. shark
    10. parent
    11. always

D 1. a
    2. b
    3. c
    4. b
    5. c
    6. b
    7. b
    8. b
    9. a. Margaret
      b. John
      c. 12

E 1. who or what
    2. the action
    3. phrases

F Underline   Circle
    2. The wind   blew harder
    3. The ship   is turning
    4. Sam   fell down
    5. Margaret   ran quickly

G Write an *S* by sentences 2, 3, 6, and 7.

H 1. before
    2. before
    3. after
    4. before
    5. before
    6. after

I 1. c
    2. d
    3. b
    4. a

J Paragraphs will vary.

Answer Key
Core Skills Reading Comprehension, Grade 3

Selection 12
pages 97–104

A
1. d
2. d
3. a
4. b
5. a
6. d
7. d
8. b
9. c
10. b
11. a
12. d

B
1. 21
2. 3
3. 4
4. 70
5. a. Columbus's
   b. 277

C Day Times: morning, dawn, noon, sunrise
Night Times: evening, darkness, bedtime, midnight

D
1. h
2. d
3. e
4. b
5. f
6. c
7. a
8. g

E
1. c
2. a
3. b
4. d
5. b
6. c

F
1. now
2. long ago
3. now
4. now
5. now
6. long ago
7. long ago

G
1. appeared
2. breeze
3. serious
4. stirred
5. bonnet
6. darkness
7. drifted
8. several
9. enough
10. crew

H
1. b, d
2. c
3. a, e
4. d

Selection 13
pages 105–112

A
1. c
2. a
3. b
4. d
5. c
6. a
7. d
8. c
9. c
10. b
11. c
12. d
13. b

B Completed outlines should read:
How Bees Are Like Human Beings
  I. Live in groups
    A. Work together
    B. Have their own jobs
  II. Have many enemies
    A. Skunks
    B. Bears
    C. Sickness

C
1. d
2. g
3. f
4. b
5. c
6. e
7. a

D Completed outline should read:
Why Turtles Have Lived So Long
  I. Live almost anywhere
    A. On land
    B. In fresh water
    C. In salt water
  II. Eat many things
    A. Dead fish
    B. Insects and berries
    C. Freshwater plants
  III. Protect themselves
    A. Have a bad smell
    B. Hide in their shells
    C. Snap at enemies

E
1. swamps
2. million
3. enemies
4. protect
5. human beings
6. eagle
7. crush
8. damp
9. swift
10. snap

Selection 14
pages 113–120

A
1. d
2. b
3. d
4. a
5. d
6. c
7. a
8. b
9. c
10. a
11. b

B Students should write evaporation next to 1, 3, 4, and 6.

C
1. c
2. a
3. c

D
1. b, c
2. e
3. a
4. d
5. c, b

E
1. pals
2. empty
3. bubble
4. experiment
5. secret
6. proof
7. interesting
8. taste

Selection 15
pages 121–128

A
1. b
2. d
3. b
4. b
5. d
6. b
7. c
8. b
9. d
10. c

B Mark an *X* by sentences 2, 5, and 6.

C
a. 1, 2, 3, 4
b. 2, 3
c. 1
d. 1, 3, 4
e. 1, 4
f. 2
g. 1
h. 2, 3, 4
i. 3, 4
j. 2
k. 1

D 1. Dr. Garza
2. Dr. Stern
3. Dr. Serra
4. Dr. Morgan
5. Dr. Grove
6. Dr. Yee

E 1. discovery
2. village
3. teased
4. spear
5. listened
6. yesterday
7. tunnel
8. explore
9. promised
10. cave-in
11. pasture
12. lizard
13. doorbell

Selection 16
pages 129–134

A 1. b
2. a
3. c
4. b
5. b
6. d
7. b
8. a

B 1. ranger
2. burning
3. stamp
4. camping
5. finish
6. sparks
7. tent
8. careful

C Make sure the directions for marking the map were followed.

D 1. NS   8. S
2. S   9. NS
3. S   10. S
4. NS   11. NS
5. S   12. S
6. NS   13. NS
7. NS   14. S

E 1. a   4. b
2. b   5. c
3. a   6. c

Selection 17
pages 135–140

A 1. c   5. a
2. c   6. b
3. b   7. c
4. d   8. b

B 1. c
2. d
3. b
4. e
5. a

C 1. Tom
2. Mrs. Boone
3. Pam Panda

D 1. b
2. c
3. c
4. c
5. a
6. a

E 1. a
2. c
3. c

F 1. b
2. a
3. b

Skills Review: Selections 11–17
pages 141–146

A (1st) Jane and Jessie Horn
(2nd) Scott
(3rd) Gus West
(4th) Mr. Pepper
(5th) Mary Burns

B 1. at a friend's house
2. at eleven o'clock
3. by thinking
4. to take him to the doctor
5. because of the baseball diamond
6. at the last house
7. at the fourth house
8. Jane and Jessie Horn

C 1. b
2. c
3. a
4. c
5. c
6. c
7. b
8. b

D 1. equipment for school
2. how travel began
3. the cookbook

E 1. Wind can help people.
2. Wind can hurt people.

F 1. after
2. after
3. before
4. after
5. before
6. The hat was in a high place.